Essential
Mathematics

AI Foundations

Essential
Mathematics

AI Foundations

Sergio Ramírez Gallardo

Index

## Chapter 1

Introduction to Mathematics in AI

Artificial intelligence (AI) is a constantly evolving field based on various disciplines, with mathematics being one of the most crucial. In this chapter, we will explore the importance of mathematics in AI, as well as its history and the development of mathematical concepts that have enabled technological advancement in this domain.

Why is Mathematics Necessary in AI?

Mathematics is the language of scientific knowledge. In the realm of artificial intelligence, these mathematical concepts facilitate the construction, analysis, and optimization of models that seek to replicate characteristics of human intelligence. Here are some key reasons why mathematics is fundamental in AI:

- **Problem Modeling:** Many AI applications involve formulating problems in mathematical terms, allowing for a more precise description of phenomena. This includes everything from representing data to modeling decisions.

- **Efficient Algorithms:** Mathematics enables the design of efficient algorithms to process and analyze vast amounts of data. From linear algebra to optimization, these tools help create models that can learn and adapt.

- **Result Validation:** Mathematics provides methods to validate and analyze the results produced by AI models. This includes statistical techniques that allow measuring the effectiveness and accuracy of algorithms.

- **Theoretical Understanding:** Understanding the mathematical foundations brings clarity to how AI models work. This is essential not only for development but also for interpreting results and making informed decisions.

Example: Betting in Games of Chance

Imagine you are playing a game of chance and want to maximize your winnings. This is where mathematics comes into play. By using statistical concepts, you can analyze the probability of winning and find the optimal betting strategy. Just as in AI, where we use probabilistic models to make predictions, this analysis provides a solid foundation for making informed decisions.

History and Development of Mathematics in AI

Mathematics and AI have been intertwined since the beginnings of the field. A brief historical review will help us understand how this relationship has developed:

- **1950s:** In the early days of AI, mathematicians and scientists began implementing statistical methods in algorithm development. One milestone was the creation of simple neural networks, inspired by neural connections in the human brain.

- **1960s and 1970s:** There was progress in developing machine learning algorithms, based on principles of statistics and probability theory. During this period, Bayesian inference began to gain relevance as an approach to modeling uncertainty.

- **1980s:** The rise of computing allowed for more complex applications of mathematics in AI. Methods such as the gradient algorithm, derived from differential calculus, became essential for model optimization.

- **2000s and 2010s:** With the increase in computing power and the availability of large volumes of data, advanced techniques such as deep neural networks and unsupervised learning emerged as leaders in the field of AI. These models require a deep understanding of linear algebra and applied calculus.

Conclusion

The initial introduction of mathematics in artificial intelligence reveals the critical interconnection between these fields. The ability to formulate problems, design efficient algorithms, and verify results is based on mathematical tools. In the upcoming chapters, we will delve into specific concepts that form the backbone of AI, starting with linear algebra, an essential component for understanding the structure and manipulation of data in this fascinating field.

## Chapter 2

Applied Linear Algebra in AI

Linear algebra is an essential branch of mathematics that studies vectors, matrices, and the various operations that can be performed on them. In the context of artificial intelligence (AI), linear algebra turns out to be a fundamental tool, as many algorithms that underlie machine learning and neural networks depend on these concepts. Throughout this chapter, we will delve into the basic elements of linear algebra and their applications in AI.

Vectors and Vector Spaces

What is a Vector?

A vector can be understood as a mathematical entity that has both magnitude and direction. From a geometric perspective, a vector can be visualized as an arrow pointing from one point of origin to another point in an n-dimensional space. However, mathematically, a vector can be represented as an ordered list of numbers. For example, in a three-dimensional space, a vector can be expressed as:

$$\mathbf{v} = \begin{pmatrix} 3 \\ 4 \\ 5 \end{pmatrix}$$

In this case, each number in the vector is called a component and can be interpreted as a coordinate in space. Vectors are particularly useful in AI for efficiently representing data.

Vector Spaces

A vector space is defined as a set of vectors that can be combined through addition and scalar multiplication, adhering to certain mathematical properties. An example of a vector space is the set of all two-dimensional vectors, where we can add two vectors and multiply them by a scalar. This concept is vital in AI, as it helps us understand how different features of data can be combined.

Application in AI

In the field of AI, vectors are used to represent datasets. For example, an image can be flattened and represented as a vector where each component corresponds to a pixel. This vector representation allows machine learning algorithms to process and analyze data more efficiently.

Matrices and Matrix Operations

What is a Matrix?

A matrix is a rectangular structure of numbers organized in rows and columns. For example, a matrix A of size $m \times n$ can be represented as:

$$A = \begin{pmatrix} a_{11} & a_{12} & \cdots & a_{1n} \\ a_{21} & a_{22} & \cdots & a_{2n} \\ \vdots & \vdots & \ddots & \vdots \\ a_{m1} & a_{m2} & \cdots & a_{mn} \end{pmatrix}$$

Matrix Operations

There are various operations that can be performed with matrices, including:

- **Matrix Addition:** Two matrices can be added only if they have the same dimensions. The addition is performed element-wise.

$$C = A + B$$

If A and B are matrices of the same dimension, the element located at the position (i, j) of the resulting matrix C will be $c_{ij} = a_{ij} + b_{ij}$.

- **Matrix Multiplication:** The multiplication of one matrix by another requires that the number of columns in the first matrix equals the number of rows in the second. If A is of size $m \times n$ and B is of size $n \times p$, the product $C = A \times B$ will be of size $m \times p$.

The entry c_{ij} in the resulting matrix C is computed as:

$$c_{ij} = \sum_{k=1}^{n} a_{ik} b_{kj}$$

- **Matrix Transposition:** The transposition of a matrix involves swapping its rows for columns. A transposed matrix is represented as A^T.

Application in AI

Matrices are fundamental in AI, as they allow for simultaneous calculations over large datasets. During the training of neural networks, both the input data and the model weights are represented as matrices. Matrix operations are crucial for calculating the model output and for updating the weights during optimization.

Example in Python

The following example illustrates how to perform matrix operations using the NumPy library, which is essential for numerical computations in Python:

```python
import numpy as np

# Define two matrices
A = np.array([[1, 2], [3, 4]])
B = np.array([[5, 6], [7, 8]])

# Matrix addition
C = A + B

# Matrix multiplication (product)
D = np.dot(A, B)

print("Matrix Addition:\n", C)
print("Matrix Multiplication:\n", D)
```

Eigenvalues and Eigenvectors

What are Eigenvalues and Eigenvectors?

Eigenvalues and eigenvectors are key concepts in linear algebra that characterize special properties of matrices. For a square matrix A, a vector $\mathbf{v}$ is called an eigenvector if there exists a scalar λ such that:

$$A\mathbf{v} = \lambda\mathbf{v}$$

In this equation, λ is the eigenvalue associated with the eigenvector $\mathbf{v}$. This means that when the vector $\mathbf{v}$ is transformed by the matrix A, the result is simply the vector $\mathbf{v}$ scaled by λ.

Significance and Applications in AI

The analysis of eigenvalues and eigenvectors is crucial in dimensionality reduction techniques, such as Principal Component Analysis (PCA). PCA identifies the directions in which the data varies the most, thereby allowing for a more compact and efficient representation of the data, which is especially useful in image processing and feature extraction.

Example of Eigenvalue and Eigenvector Calculation in Python

```python
# Define a matrix
matrix = np.array([[4, 2], [1, 3]])

# Calculate eigenvalues and eigenvectors
```

```
5  eigenvalues, eigenvectors = np.linalg.eig(matrix)
6
7  print("Eigenvalues:", eigenvalues)
8  print("Eigenvectors:\n", eigenvectors)
```

Applications of Linear Algebra in AI

Linear algebra provides the mathematical tools necessary for nearly all algorithms in AI. Some applications include:

- **Neural Networks:** In neural networks, the flow of information across layers is represented through matrices. The weights and inputs are organized in matrices, and the training process involves matrix operations that enable weight adjustment.

- **Clustering and Segmentation:** Algorithms such as K-means utilize Euclidean distances, which are calculated through linear algebra operations between vectors, to classify data into different groups.

- **Dimensionality Reduction:** Techniques like PCA simplify complex datasets, thereby optimizing the analysis and learning processes.

Conclusion

Linear algebra is an essential pillar in artificial intelligence, providing the necessary tools for manipulating and analyzing data in multiple dimensions. A deep understanding of vectors, matrices, and their operations allows developers to design and optimize machine learning models that are fundamental in the world of AI. As we progress through this book, we will explore more concepts and techniques that complement the use of linear algebra in this exciting field.

## Chapter 3

Probability and Statistics for Machine Learning

Probability and statistics are fundamental disciplines in the field of artificial intelligence and, in particular, in machine learning. The ability to model uncertainty and make inferences from data is essential for building models that can make informed decisions. This chapter will explore the basic concepts of probability and statistics, as well as their application in machine learning.

Fundamental Concepts of Probability

Probability is a numerical measure of uncertainty expressed on a scale from 0 to 1. An event with a probability of 0 is impossible, while an event with a probability of 1 is certain. To understand probability, it is essential to familiarize oneself with some key concepts:

Sample Space

The sample space is the set of all possible outcomes of a random experiment. For example, when rolling a die, the sample space would be:

$$S = \{1, 2, 3, 4, 5, 6\}$$

In this case, when rolling a six-sided die, there are six possible outcomes, and each one has the same probability of occurring if the die is fair.

Event

An event is a subset of the sample space. For example, the event of rolling an even number on the die is:

$$E = \{2, 4, 6\}$$

Here, the event includes three outcomes (2, 4, and 6) that satisfy a specific condition. Each event has a probability that can be calculated.

Probability of an Event

The probability of an event E can be calculated as:

$$P(E) = \frac{\text{number of favorable outcomes}}{\text{total number of possible outcomes}}$$

For our event E:

$$P(E) = \frac{3}{6} = \frac{1}{2}$$

This indicates that there is a 50% chance of rolling an even number on the die.

Conditional Probability

Conditional probability refers to the probability of an event given that another event has already occurred. It is expressed as:

$$P(A \mid B) = \frac{P(A \cap B)}{P(B)}$$

This means that the probability of A given B is equal to the probability that both events occur, divided by the probability of event B.

Example: Rolling Two Dice

Suppose we roll two dice and are interested in event A: "the sum of the two dice equals 7". Furthermore, let's define event B: "the first die is 3".

To calculate $P(A \mid B)$, we need to find the probability of getting a sum of 7 given that the first die is 3:

1. If the first die is 3, the only way for the sum to be 7 is if the second die is 4.

2. The sample space for the second die remains {1, 2, 3, 4, 5, 6}.

Thus, the probability that the sum is 7 given that the first die is 3 is:

$$P(A \mid B) = \frac{1}{6}$$

This indicates that there is about a 16.67% chance of getting a sum of 7 assuming the first die is 3.

Bayes' Theorem

Bayes' Theorem is a fundamental tool in statistical inference that allows for the inversion of probabilities. It is formulated as:

$$P(A \mid B) = \frac{P(B \mid A) \cdot P(A)}{P(B)}$$

This theorem is frequently used in machine learning models, especially when dealing with uncertain data and making inferences from data.

Example: Disease Detection

Imagine we are interested in a medical diagnosis. Suppose that:

- The prior probability that a patient has a disease A is 0.01 (1%).

- If the patient has the disease, the probability that the test is positive $P(B \mid A)$ is 0.9 (90%).

- If the patient does not have the disease, the probability that the test is positive $P(B \mid \neg A)$ is 0.05 (5%).

We want to calculate the probability that the patient actually has the disease given that the test was positive $P(A \mid B)$.

First, we will apply Bayes' theorem:

1. The total probability that the test is positive $P(B)$ can be calculated using the law of total probability:

$$P(B) = P(B \mid A) \cdot P(A) + P(B \mid \neg A) \cdot P(\neg A)$$

Let's calculate it:

- $P(\neg A) = 1 - P(A) = 1 - 0.01 = 0.99$

Then,

$$P(B) = (0.9 \cdot 0.01) + (0.05 \cdot 0.99) = 0.009 + 0.0495 = 0.0585$$

2. Now we use Bayes' theorem:

$$P(A \mid B) = \frac{P(B \mid A) \cdot P(A)}{P(B)} = \frac{0.9 \cdot 0.01}{0.0585} \approx 0.154$$

This means that despite the positive test result, there is about a 15.4% chance that the patient actually has the disease. This result underscores the limitations of tests and the importance of considering prior probabilities.

Random Variables and Expectations

A random variable is a function that assigns a real number to each outcome of a random experiment. Random variables can be discrete or continuous.

Discrete Random Variables

Discrete random variables take a finite or countable number of values. For example, when rolling a die, the random variable X representing the result can take the values 1, 2, 3, 4, 5, or 6. The probability function of X can be expressed as:

$$P(X = x) = \text{probability that } X \text{ takes the value } x$$

Example: Rolling a Die

If X is the outcome of rolling a die, we can define the probability function:

- $P(X = 1) = \frac{1}{6}$
- $P(X = 2) = \frac{1}{6}$
- $P(X = 3) = \frac{1}{6}$
- $P(X = 4) = \frac{1}{6}$
- $P(X = 5) = \frac{1}{6}$
- $P(X = 6) = \frac{1}{6}$

Mathematical Expectation

The mathematical expectation or expected value of a random variable X, denoted as $E(X)$, is a weighted average value of all possibilities. For a discrete random variable, it is calculated as:

$$E(X) = \sum_i x_i \cdot P(X = x_i)$$

Using our die example:

$$E(X) = (1 \cdot \tfrac{1}{6}) + (2 \cdot \tfrac{1}{6}) + (3 \cdot \tfrac{1}{6}) + (4 \cdot \tfrac{1}{6}) + (5 \cdot \tfrac{1}{6}) + (6 \cdot \tfrac{1}{6})$$

$$E(X) = \frac{1+2+3+4+5+6}{6} = \frac{21}{6} = 3.5$$

This indicates that the expected average value when rolling the die is 3.5.

Conclusion

Probability and statistics are fundamental in the field of artificial intelligence and machine learning. Understanding these concepts not only allows for the construction of more robust and accurate models but also helps interpret the results meaningfully. The mathematical and statistical tools we have explored are essential for handling uncertainty in data and obtaining key inferences in various situations. As we advance in this series, it is crucial to keep these principles in mind to correctly apply more advanced techniques in AI. In the next chapter, we will explore probability distributions that play a crucial role in modeling uncertainty in data.

## Chapter 4

Probability Distributions

Probability distributions are fundamental in the study of statistics and play a crucial role in the development of artificial intelligence (AI) and machine learning models. These distributions allow us to understand and represent variability in data and facilitate the modeling of random phenomena. In this chapter, we explore different types of probability distributions, their characteristics, and practical applications.

Discrete Distributions

Discrete distributions are used to model events that can take on a finite or countable number of values. This includes distributions that describe the number of successes in a fixed number of trials or the frequency of events in a given time interval.

Binomial Distribution

The binomial distribution is one of the most commonly used discrete distributions. It applies to experiments that meet the following conditions:

- There is a fixed number of trials n.

- Each trial has only two possible outcomes, commonly referred to as "success" and "failure."

- The probability of success, p, remains constant for each trial.

- The trials are independent of each other.

The probability function for the binomial distribution is expressed as:

$$P(X = k) = \binom{n}{k} p^k (1 - p)^{n-k}$$

where:

- $P(X = k)$ is the probability of obtaining k successes in n trials.

- $\binom{n}{k}$ is the binomial coefficient, which calculates the number of ways to choose k successes from n trials, given by the formula:

$$\binom{n}{k} = \frac{n!}{k!(n-k)!}$$

Example: Tossing a Coin

Suppose we toss a fair coin 10 times and want to calculate the probability of obtaining exactly 3 heads.

Here, $n = 10$, $k = 3$, and $p = 0.5$.

We calculate $P(X = 3)$:

$$P(X = 3) = \binom{10}{3}(0.5)^3(0.5)^{10-3}$$

First, we calculate the binomial coefficient:

$$\binom{10}{3} = \frac{10!}{3!(10-3)!} = \frac{10 \times 9 \times 8}{3 \times 2 \times 1} = 120$$

Substituting into the formula:

$$P(X = 3) = 120 \cdot (0.5)^3 \cdot (0.5)^7 = 120 \cdot \frac{1}{1024} \approx 0.1172$$

This indicates that there is approximately an 11.72% probability of obtaining exactly 3 heads when tossing the coin 10 times.

Poisson Distribution

The Poisson distribution is used to model the number of events that occur in a fixed interval of time or space. This distribution is particularly useful when events are rare or occur independently.

The probability function for the Poisson distribution is expressed as:

$$P(X = k) = \frac{\lambda^k e^{-\lambda}}{k!}$$

where:

- λ is the average number of events that occur in an interval.

- k is the number of observed events.

Example: Arrivals of Customers at a Restaurant

Imagine a restaurant receives an average of 3 customers per hour. Here, $\lambda = 3$ and we want to find the probability that exactly 2 customers arrive in one hour.

$$P(X = 2) = \frac{3^2 e^{-3}}{2!} = \frac{9e^{-3}}{2} \approx \frac{9 \cdot 0.0498}{2} \approx 0.224$$

This means there is a 22.4% probability that exactly 2 customers will arrive in one hour.

Continuous Distributions

Continuous distributions are used to model events that can take on an infinite number of values within an interval. Unlike discrete distributions, probabilities in continuous distributions are represented through probability density functions (PDF).

Normal Distribution

The normal distribution, or Gaussian distribution, is one of the most important distributions in statistics. It is characterized by its bell shape, defined by two parameters: the mean μ and the standard deviation σ.

The probability density function for a random variable X that follows a normal distribution is expressed as:

$$f(x) = \frac{1}{\sigma\sqrt{2\pi}}e^{-\frac{(x-\mu)^2}{2\sigma^2}}$$

Example: Height of People

Suppose the heights of adults in a population follow a normal distribution with a mean $\mu = 170$ cm and a standard deviation $\sigma = 10$ cm. If we wanted to calculate the probability that a randomly selected person is taller than 180 cm, we first need to calculate the z-score:

$$z = \frac{x-\mu}{\sigma} = \frac{180-170}{10} = 1$$

Then, we consult the standard normal distribution table to find $P(Z > 1)$. This is approximately 15.87%.

Exponential Distribution

The exponential distribution describes the time until an event occurs in a continuous process. It is commonly used in waiting time processes and reliability analysis. Its density function is expressed as:

$$f(x; \lambda) = \lambda e^{-\lambda x} \quad \text{for } x \geq 0$$

where λ is the rate of events per unit time.

Example: Waiting Time to be Served in a Restaurant

If a restaurant has an average waiting time of 5 minutes, the rate λ would be $\frac{1}{5} = 0.2$ per minute. The probability that a customer waits less than 3 minutes can be calculated by integrating the density function:

$$P(X < 3) = \int_0^3 0.2 e^{-0.2x} dx \approx 0.4513$$

This indicates that there is a 45.13% probability of being served in less than 3 minutes.

Applications of Probability Distributions in AI

Probability distributions are fundamental in the development of machine learning models. Some of their applications include:

- **Probabilistic Models:** Algorithms such as Naive Bayes are modeled using probability distributions to classify data based on observed features.

- **Statistical Inference:** In supervised learning, distributions are used to model the relationship between independent and dependent variables, helping make predictions.

- **Bayesianism:** Bayesian inference allows for the updating of beliefs about models by observing new data, using probability distributions to represent prior information and likelihoods.

Conclusion

Probability distributions play an essential role in the modeling and analysis of data in the field of artificial intelligence. Understanding the characteristics and applications of discrete and continuous distributions provides a solid foundation for working with random phenomena and developing robust machine learning models. With this knowledge, the reader will be able to tackle more complex problems in applied statistics and their relationship with artificial intelligence in the subsequent chapters.

## Chapter 5

Bayesian Inference

Bayesian inference is a powerful tool in the field of statistics and artificial intelligence (AI) that allows us to update our beliefs about a model as new evidence is incorporated. This chapter will explore the fundamentals of Bayesian inference, its importance in decision-making, and how it is applied in AI models.

Fundamentals of Bayesian Inference

Bayesian inference is based on Bayes' Theorem, which is used to calculate the probability of an event given another event. The theorem is formulated as follows:

$$P(A \mid B) = \frac{P(B \mid A) \cdot P(A)}{P(B)}$$

Where:

- $P(A \mid B)$: The probability that event A occurs given that event B has occurred (posterior probability).

- $P(B \mid A)$: The probability that event B occurs given that event A has occurred (likelihood).

- $P(A)$: The probability that event A occurs before having any information about B (prior probability).

- $P(B)$: The probability that event B occurs in general (normalizing probability).

Key Concepts

Prior Probability: This is the initial belief about an event or parameter before observing any evidence. For instance, if we are trying to determine whether a customer will make a purchase, our prior probability might be based on their purchase history.

Likelihood: This is the probability of observing the data given a set of parameters. It reflects how well a model fits the observed data.

Posterior Probability: This is the new probability obtained by combining the prior probability and the likelihood after observing data. This probability is used to make updated inferences about the event.

Example of Bayesian Inference

To illustrate Bayesian inference, consider a classic case: diagnosing a disease based on the result of a test.

Scenario

Suppose we have a rare disease that affects 1% of the population. A diagnostic test has a false positive rate of 5% (meaning 5% of healthy people will give a positive result) and a true positive rate of 90% (meaning

90% of sick people will give a positive result). We want to know the probability that a person has the disease given that the test result is positive.

Definition of Events

- Let A: the event that a person has the disease.
- Let B: the event that the test is positive.

We calculate the probabilities:

- $P(A) = 0.01$ (prior probability).
- $P(B \mid A) = 0.90$ (likelihood).
- $P(B \mid \neg A) = 0.05$ (the probability that the test is positive given that the person does not have the disease).
- $P(\neg A) = 0.99$ (the probability of not having the disease).

Calculation of $P(B)$

We use the law of total probability to calculate $P(B)$:

$$P(B) = P(B \mid A) \cdot P(A) + P(B \mid \neg A) \cdot P(\neg A)$$

Substituting the values:

$$P(B) = (0.90 \cdot 0.01) + (0.05 \cdot 0.99) = 0.009 + 0.0495 = 0.0585$$

Application of Bayes' Theorem

Now that we have $P(B)$, we can use Bayes' Theorem to calculate

$P(A \mid B)$:

$$P(A \mid B) = \frac{P(B \mid A) \cdot P(A)}{P(B)}$$

Substituting the values:

$$P(A \mid B) = \frac{0.90 \cdot 0.01}{0.0585} \approx 0.154$$

This means that despite the positive test result, there is approximately a 15.4% probability that the person actually has the disease. This result is surprising, as the effectiveness of the test is often overestimated.

Applications in Artificial Intelligence

Bayesian inference is particularly useful in AI for several reasons:

- **Probabilistic Modeling**: It allows for modeling uncertainty in a structured and formal manner, which is crucial when working with noisy or incomplete data.

- **Adaptive Learning**: As more data is gathered, Bayesian models automatically update, enabling continuous improvements in predictions.

- **Informed Decisions**: Bayesian models enable the calculation of the probability of various possible outcomes, aiding in decision-making under uncertainty.

Example in Machine Learning: Naive Bayes Classification

One of the simplest models that uses Bayesian inference is the Naive Bayes classifier. This classifier relies on the assumption that the features are independent of one another (hence the "naive" aspect).

Implementation in Python

Below is a basic example of how to implement a Naive Bayes classifier using the `sklearn` library. This example uses a fictional dataset.

```python
1   import numpy as np
2   import pandas as pd
3   from sklearn.model_selection import train_test_split
4   from sklearn.naive_bayes import GaussianNB
5   from sklearn.metrics import accuracy_score
6
7   # Create a fictional dataset
8   data = {
9       'age': [22, 25, 47, 35, 46, 52, 23, 43],
10      'income': [15000, 24000, 50000, 30000, 50000, 60000,
        15000, 35000],
11      'purchased': [0, 0, 1, 0, 1, 1, 0, 1]
        # 0 = Did not purchase, 1 = Purchased
12  }
13
14  df = pd.DataFrame(data)
15
16  # Separate the predictor variables and the target variable
17  X = df[['age', 'income']]
18  y = df['purchased']
19
20  # Split the dataset into training and testing sets
21  X_train, X_test, y_train, y_test = train_test_split(X, y,
        test_size=0.25, random_state=42)
22
23  # Create and train the model
24  model = GaussianNB()
25  model.fit(X_train, y_train)
26
```

```
27  # Make predictions
28  predictions = model.predict(X_test)
29
30  # Calculate the accuracy of the model
31  accuracy = accuracy_score(y_test, predictions)
32
33  print(f'Model accuracy: {accuracy * 100:.2f}%')
```

In this code, we construct a fictional dataset that follows a simple pattern, then train a Naive Bayes classification model to predict whether a customer will purchase based on their age and income. Finally, we evaluate the model's accuracy.

Comparison with Frequentist Methods

Bayesian inference is often contrasted with frequentist statistical methods in practice and interpretations. The main difference lies in how uncertainty is managed.

- **Frequentism**: Treats probabilities as long-term limits of events. For example, a probability of 60% means that in 60 out of 100 trials, the event will occur.

- **Bayesianism**: Treats probabilities as degrees of belief. Here, a probability of 60% means that, based on the evidence available, one is 60% confident of the event's occurrence.

Both approaches have their advantages and disadvantages, and the choice between them depends on the context and specific objectives of the analysis.

Conclusion

Bayesian inference provides a rigorous and flexible framework for decision-making under uncertainty, adapting to new evidence as data is gathered. Its application in artificial intelligence is broad, facilitating models that can learn and improve over time.

As the field of artificial intelligence continues to evolve, understanding Bayesian inference and its applications becomes a key skill for those wishing to work in this exciting domain. In the upcoming chapters, we will explore more advanced techniques applied in artificial intelligence, which often build on the fundamentals discussed here.

## Chapter 6

Linear and Logistic Regressions

Regression is a fundamental technique in data analysis and holds great relevance in the field of artificial intelligence (AI) and machine learning. Linear regression and logistic regression are two of the most common ways to model relationships between variables. In this chapter, we will explore both techniques, their theoretical foundations, applications, and practical examples in Python.

Linear Regression Model

What is Linear Regression?

Linear regression is a technique that models the relationship between a dependent variable and one or more independent variables using a linear equation. This approach is commonly used to predict continuous values based on observed data.

The equation of a simple linear regression (one independent variable) is expressed as follows:

$$y = \beta_0 + \beta_1 x + \epsilon$$

Where:

- y: dependent variable (what we want to predict).

- β_0: intercept of the line on the y axis.

- β_1: slope of the line, representing the change in y for each unit change in x.

- x: independent variable (input).

- ϵ: error term, reflecting the variability of y that is not explained by x.

Assumptions of Linear Regression

Before applying linear regression, it is important to ensure that certain assumptions are met:

1. **Linearity**: The relationship between the independent and dependent variables must be linear.

2. **Independence**: Observations must be independent of each other.

3. **Homoscedasticity**: The variance of the error term must be constant across different values of x.

4. **Normality**: Errors should be normally distributed.

Example of Linear Regression

Let's suppose we want to predict the price of a house based on its area in square feet. We will use a fictional dataset to illustrate what we have learned.

```python
import numpy as np
import pandas as pd
import matplotlib.pyplot as plt
from sklearn.model_selection import train_test_split
from sklearn.linear_model import LinearRegression

# Create a fictional dataset
data = {
    'area': [1500, 1600, 1700, 1800, 1900, 2000, 2100, 2200
, 2300, 2400],
    'price': [300000, 320000, 340000, 360000, 380000,
400000, 420000, 440000, 460000, 480000]
}

df = pd.DataFrame(data)

# Separate independent and dependent variables
X = df[['area']]   # independent variable
y = df['price']    # dependent variable

# Split the dataset into training and testing sets
X_train, X_test, y_train, y_test = train_test_split(X, y,
    test_size=0.2, random_state=42)

# Create and train the linear regression model
model = LinearRegression()
model.fit(X_train, y_train)

```

```
26   # Make predictions
27   y_pred = model.predict(X_test)
28
29   # Visualization of results
30   plt.figure(figsize=(10, 6))
31   plt.scatter(X, y, color='blue', label='Observed Data')
32   plt.plot(X_test, y_pred, color='red', linewidth=2, label=
     'Regression Line')
33   plt.title('Linear Regression: House Prices')
34   plt.xlabel('Area (square feet)')
35   plt.ylabel('Price ($)')
36   plt.legend()
37   plt.show()
38
39   # Display the coefficients
40   print(f'Intercept: {model.intercept_}')
41   print(f'Slope: {model.coef_[0]}')
```

In this example, we generate a dataset relating the area of houses to their prices. Then, we split the data into training and testing sets, train the linear regression model, and finally visualize the regression line overlaid on the observed data.

Evaluation of the Linear Regression Model

Once a linear regression model has been trained, it is essential to evaluate its performance using appropriate metrics:

- **Mean Squared Error (MSE)**: Measures the average of the squared errors, showing how close the predictions are to the actual value.

$$MSE = \frac{1}{n} \sum_{i=1}^{n} (y_i - \hat{y}_i)^2$$

- **Coefficient of Determination (R^2)**: Indicates how well the variability of the dependent variable is explained by the independent variables. Its value can range from 0 to 1, where a value closer to 1 suggests a better fit.

Logistic Regression

What is Logistic Regression?

Logistic regression is a modeling technique used to predict the outcome of a categorical variable (binary or multiple) from one or more independent variables. Instead of predicting continuous values, logistic regression predicts the probability of belonging to a specific class.

The logistic function that models this relationship is defined as:

$$p = \frac{1}{1+e^{-z}}$$

where:

$$z = \beta_0 + \beta_1 x_1 + \beta_2 x_2 + \ldots + \beta_n x_n$$

and:

- p: probability that the event occurs (e.g., that a customer buys a product).

- z: linear combination of the independent variables.

- e: base of the natural logarithm.

The final formula for logistic regression predicts the probability of the positive class.

Assumptions of Logistic Regression

Just like with linear regression, logistic regression has certain assumptions:

1. **Linear Relationship**: Logistic regression assumes there is a linear relationship between the independent variables and the log of the odds ratios.

2. **Independence**: Observations must be independent of each other.

3. **No Multicollinearity**: The independent variables should not be highly correlated with each other.

Example of Logistic Regression

Let's imagine we have a dataset about whether a customer made a purchase based on their age and income.

```python
from sklearn.datasets import make_classification
from sklearn.linear_model import LogisticRegression
from sklearn.metrics import accuracy_score,
confusion_matrix
import seaborn as sns

# Create a fictional dataset for classification
X, y = make_classification(n_samples=1000, n_features=2,
    n_classes=2, n_clusters_per_class=1, random_state=42)

# Split the dataset
X_train, X_test, y_train, y_test = train_test_split(X, y,
    test_size=0.2, random_state=42)

# Create and train the logistic regression model
logit_model = LogisticRegression()
```

```
14  logit_model.fit(X_train, y_train)
15
16  # Make predictions
17  y_pred_logit = logit_model.predict(X_test)
18
19  # Calculate accuracy
20  logit_accuracy = accuracy_score(y_test, y_pred_logit)
21  print(f'Logistic Regression Accuracy: {logit_accuracy * 100
    :.2f}%')
22
23  # Create confusion matrix
24  cm = confusion_matrix(y_test, y_pred_logit)
25
26  # Visualize confusion matrix
27  plt.figure(figsize=(8, 6))
28  sns.heatmap(cm, annot=True, fmt='d', cmap='Blues',
      xticklabels=['No Purchase', 'Purchase'], yticklabels=[
      'No Purchase', 'Purchase'])
29  plt.title('Confusion Matrix: Logistic Regression')
30  plt.ylabel('Actual Label')
31  plt.xlabel('Predicted Label')
32  plt.show()
```

In this example, we use the `make_classification` method to create a simulated dataset. After splitting our data, we train a logistic regression model and measure its accuracy using a confusion matrix, which represents the model's performance in correctly identifying purchases.

Evaluation of the Logistic Regression Model

Just like linear regression, it is important to evaluate the performance of a logistic regression model using appropriate metrics:

- **Accuracy**: The proportion of true positives and negatives relative to all predictions made.

$$Accuracy = \frac{TP+TN}{TP+TN+FP+FN}$$

- **Recall**: The proportion of true positives relative to the sum of true positives and false negatives.

$$Recall = \frac{TP}{TP+FN}$$

- **F1-score**: A metric that combines precision and recall.

$$F1 = 2 \cdot \frac{Accuracy \cdot Recall}{Accuracy + Recall}$$

- **ROC Curve and AUC**: A graph that shows the relationship between the true positive rate and the false positive rate at various cutoff thresholds.

Conclusion

Linear regression and logistic regression are powerful tools in data analysis and are widely used in the field of artificial intelligence. Understanding these models and their proper application allows practitioners to build effective predictive models that can be interpreted and evaluated clearly. In the following chapters, we will continue exploring advanced data analysis techniques that complement the tools discussed here.

## Chapter 7

Analysis of Variance and Correlations

Analysis of variance (ANOVA) and correlations are two fundamental statistical concepts that play a crucial role in the field of artificial intelligence and machine learning. They allow for understanding the relationship between variables and assessing whether these relationships are significant. In this chapter, we will explore ANOVA and correlations in depth, as well as their practical applications in data analysis.

Introduction to ANOVA

Analysis of variance (ANOVA) is a statistical technique that allows for comparing the means of two or more groups to determine if at least one of the groups is significantly different from the others. It is commonly used in experiments where the effect of one or more independent variables (factors) on a dependent variable (response) is investigated.

Types of ANOVA

There are several types of ANOVA, but the most common are:

- **One-way ANOVA**: Used when there is a single independent variable and the means of more than two groups are compared. For example, ANOVA could be used to evaluate the effect of different doses of a medication on blood pressure.

- **Two-way ANOVA**: Used when there are two independent variables and one wants to evaluate their effect on the dependent variable, as well as the interaction between them. For example, it could be used to analyze how diet type (variable 1) and exercise (variable 2) influence weight loss.

Hypotheses in ANOVA

The hypotheses in ANOVA are formulated as follows:

- **Null Hypothesis (H_0)**: The means of all groups are equal.

- **Alternative Hypothesis (H_a)**: At least one of the means is different.

ANOVA Calculation

The procedure for calculating ANOVA involves the following steps:

1. **Calculate the mean of each group.**

2. **Calculate the overall mean.**

3. **Calculate the sum of squares between groups (SSB) and the sum of squares within groups (SSW).**

4. **Calculate the degrees of freedom.**

5. **Calculate the mean squares.**

6. **Calculate the F value** using the ratio of the mean squares and finally compare it to a critical value from an F table to determine whether to reject the null hypothesis.

ANOVA Example in Python

To illustrate the concept of ANOVA, we will use a fictional dataset containing information about the grades of students in three different groups using different study methods.

```python
1   import pandas as pd
2   import numpy as np
3   import scipy.stats as stats
4   import matplotlib.pyplot as plt
5
6   # Create a fictional dataset
7   data = {
8       'study_method': np.repeat(['Traditional', 'Online',
        'Self-study'], 30),
9       'grade': np.concatenate([
10          np.random.normal(75, 10, 30),  # Traditional Method
11          np.random.normal(80, 10, 30),  # Online Method
12          np.random.normal(70, 10, 30)   # Self-study Method
13      ])
14  }
15
16  df = pd.DataFrame(data)
17
18  # Apply one-way ANOVA
19  anova_result = stats.f_oneway(
```

```
20        df['grade'][df['study_method'] == 'Traditional'],
21        df['grade'][df['study_method'] == 'Online'],
22        df['grade'][df['study_method'] == 'Self-study']
23  )
24
25  print(f'F Value: {anova_result.statistic}, P-value: {
     anova_result.pvalue}')
```

In this example, we generate a dataset with grades for three groups of students employing different study methods. We apply one-way ANOVA to determine if there is any significant difference in the average grade among the groups. The resulting p value will indicate whether we can reject the null hypothesis.

Results Interpretation

If the p value is less than a predefined significance level (e.g., 0.05), we reject the null hypothesis. This suggests that at least one of the study methods has a different effect on student grades.

Correlation

Correlation is a statistical measure that expresses the magnitude and direction of a linear relationship between two variables. It is used to determine if there is an association between them and to what extent.

Pearson Correlation Coefficient

The Pearson correlation coefficient is the most commonly used and is denoted as r. The value of r ranges from -1 to 1:

- $r = 1$: Perfect positive correlation.

- $r = -1$: Perfect negative correlation.

- $r = 0$: No correlation.

The formula for calculating the Pearson correlation coefficient is:

$$r = \frac{\sum(x_i - \bar{x})(y_i - \bar{y})}{\sqrt{\sum(x_i - \bar{x})^2 \sum(y_i - \bar{y})^2}}$$

Where:

- x_i and y_i are the values of the variables,

- $\bar{x}$ and $\bar{y}$ are the means of x and y.

Correlation Example in Python

Let's analyze the correlation between the number of hours studied and the academic performance of students using the following code:

```python
1  # Create a fictional dataset
2  np.random.seed(42)
3  study_hours = np.random.randint(1, 10, 100)
4  performance = study_hours * 10 + np.random.normal(0, 5, 100
   )  # Positive correlation
5
6  # Calculate the Pearson correlation coefficient
7  correlation = np.corrcoef(study_hours, performance)[0, 1]
8
9  print(f'Pearson Correlation Coefficient: {correlation:.2f}'
   )
10
11 # Visualization
12 plt.scatter(study_hours, performance)
```

```
13  plt.title(
    'Relationship between Study Hours and Academic Performance'
    )
14  plt.xlabel('Study Hours')
15  plt.ylabel('Academic Performance')
16  plt.axhline(y=np.mean(performance), color='r', linestyle=
    '--')
17  plt.axvline(x=np.mean(study_hours), color='g', linestyle=
    '--')
18  plt.show()
```

In this example, we generate a dataset that relates study hours to academic performance. We calculate the Pearson correlation coefficient and visualize the relationship between the two variables in a scatter plot. The red and green lines represent the means of performance and study hours, respectively.

Results Interpretation of Correlation

A correlation coefficient close to 1 indicates a strong positive correlation, while a coefficient close to -1 indicates a strong negative correlation. A coefficient near 0 suggests that there is no linear relationship between the variables.

Specific Cases

- **Correlation $r = 1$**: Imagine we have two related variables, such as temperature in degrees Celsius (x) and degrees Fahrenheit (y). The relationship between these two can be expressed linearly as $y = 1.8x + 32$. In this case, as x increases, y will always increase at a constant rate, resulting in a perfect positive correlation.

- **Correlation** $r = -1$: Consider a scenario where we have two variables: the time spent in physical activity (x) and body weight (y) in a group following a very strict weight loss plan. As the time of physical activity increases, body weight decreases in a perfectly inverse relationship, resulting in a perfect negative correlation.

- **Correlation** $r = 0$: A case of zero correlation might be found between the variables "eye color" and "height." These attributes of individuals have no inherent relationship, even though both are distributed within the population. The absence of a linear pattern in the resulting scatter plot indicates that there is no correlation between these two variables.

Correlation vs Causality

It is essential to emphasize that correlation does not imply causation. Two variables may be correlated without one effectively causing the other. This confusion is common in data analysis and can lead to misinterpretations. Let's examine some reasons contributing to this confusion.

Examples of Confusion between Correlation and Causality

1. **Hidden Variables**: In many cases, a third variable may be influencing both observed variables. For example, it has been observed that there is a direct correlation between ice cream consumption and drowning deaths. However, the hidden variable here is temperature; on hot days, people tend to consume more ice cream and also swim more, increasing the risk of drowning. The correlation between the two is merely a coincidence influenced by the third variable.

2. **Coincidences**: Sometimes, two variables may show correlations

simply due to absolute chance. For example, if we studied the relationship between the number of people using umbrellas and the decreased sales of churros, we might find a correlation. However, this does not mean that the use of umbrellas causes people to stop buying churros. Rain could be the variable that affects both.

3. **Feedback Effects**: In some systems, correlations may arise from a feedback effect. For instance, increased use of social media might correlate with decreased attention spans, but it could also be the case that decreased attention leads to more social media use, creating a vicious cycle.

4. **Directional Causality**: In certain cases, we may have a correlation where one variable causes changes in another, but the opposite influence may also be present. For example, the relationship between physical activity and mental health: exercising may improve mental health, but at the same time, individuals with good mental health may be more motivated to exercise.

Conclusion on Correlation vs Causality

When analyzing the correlation between variables, it is vital to be cautious and consider other factors that may influence the observed results. The simplicity of correlation should not lead to hasty conclusions about causation. A deeper analysis and proper experimental design are necessary to establish causal relationships.

Conclusion

Analysis of variance and correlation are essential tools in statistics that allow researchers to explore relationships between variables. ANOVA helps to determine whether there are statistically significant differences between the means of different groups, while correlation measures the strength and direction of the linear relationship between two variables.

In the context of artificial intelligence, these techniques are fundamental for understanding and modeling data. They provide a framework for analyzing and making informed decisions based on the data structure. As we progress through this book, knowledge of ANOVA and correlations will be valuable for tackling more complex problems in machine learning and data analysis.

## Chapter 8

Mathematical Optimization Methods

Mathematical optimization represents a fundamental field both in theory and practice within artificial intelligence (AI) and machine learning. It involves finding the best value (maximum or minimum) for an objective function while satisfying certain constraints. This chapter will explore the basic concepts of optimization, the methods used, and their applications in AI.

Introduction to Optimization

Optimization can be defined as the process of making something as effective, perfect, or useful as possible. In AI, this process is carried out to minimize or maximize certain functions, which may measure error, cost, or some other relevant metric. The culmination of optimization is finding the ideal point that maximizes the accuracy of a predictive model or minimizes an associated cost.

Types of Optimization Problems

Optimization problems can be classified into various categories:

- **Unconstrained Optimization**: This is a problem where the goal is to maximize or minimize an objective function without constraints on the variables. For example, finding the optimal values of a set of parameters in a linear regression model.

- **Constrained Optimization**: Here, the objective function is maximized or minimized while subject to several constraints. These constraints can be equalities or inequalities. A common example of this is linear programming.

- **Convex Optimization**: This type of optimization refers to problems where the objective function is convex, meaning that any line connecting two points on the function does not lie above the curve. Convex problems are easy to solve and guarantee that any minimum found is, in fact, the global minimum.

- **Non-Convex Optimization**: In contrast, in non-convex problems, a function may have multiple local maxima and minima, complicating the situation. Here, optimization techniques must deal with multiple peaks, which may not guarantee that a global minimum is achieved.

Fundamentals of Optimization

Objective Function

The objective function is the central point of an optimization problem. It is defined as a function $f(x)$ that one wishes to minimize or maximize. The variables of interest x are adjusted to find the optimal value of this function.

Constraints

Constraints are expressed in the form of equations or inequalities that the solution must satisfy. For example, if one wishes to maximize production under the limitation of material and time resources, the constraints must be appropriately established.

Example of Objective Function and Constraints

Consider a small manufacturer producing two products x_1 and x_2. The objective function could be given by maximizing the profits from selling these products:

$$Maximize \quad z = 5x_1 + 3x_2$$

Subject to the following constraints:

$$\begin{align*} x_1 + 2x_2 & \leq 8 \quad \text{(Resource availability)} \\ 2x_1 + x_2 & \leq 10 \quad \text{(Production time)} \\ x_1, x_2 & \geq 0 \quad \text{(Non-negativity)} \end{align*}$$

Optimization Methods

There are a variety of optimization methods employed, and below we will explore some of the most common ones used in artificial intelligence.

Gradient Method

The gradient method is a widely used optimization technique, particularly in the context of machine learning. This method seeks to minimize the objective function iteratively, using information from the gradient (the derivative) of the function.

How It Works

1. **Initialization**: Start with initial values of the variables θ.

2. **Gradient Calculation**: Calculate the gradient of the function $f(x)$ at the current point, which indicates the direction of greatest increase.

3. **Update Variables**: Adjust the values of the variables in the direction opposite to the gradient to descend on the function, following the update rule:

$$\theta = \theta - \alpha \nabla f(\theta)$$

Where α is the learning rate, a parameter that controls the magnitude of the step taken in each iteration.

4. **Repeat**: This process is repeated until convergence is reached or until a predefined criterion is met, such as a maximum number of iterations.

Example in Python

Below is a simple example of optimization using the gradient method on a quadratic function:

```python
import numpy as np

# Define the objective function and its derivative
def f(x):
    return x**2 + 3*x + 2
```

```
6
7  def df(x):
8      return 2*x + 3
9
10 # Optimization parameters
11 x_init = 0  # Initial value
12 alpha = 0.1  # Learning rate
13 tolerance = 1e-6  # Convergence criterion
14 max_iter = 100  # Maximum number of iterations
15
16 x = x_init
17 for i in range(max_iter):
18     gradient = df(x)
19     x_new = x - alpha * gradient
20     if abs(x_new - x) < tolerance:
21         break
22     x = x_new
23
24 print(f'Minimum found at x = {x}, where f(x) = {f(x)}')
```

Newton's Method

Newton's method is another important approach in optimization, especially for nonlinear problems. This method uses information about the objective function by calculating the second derivative (the Hessian matrix). Since Newton's method considers the curvature of the function, it converges more rapidly than the gradient method.

How It Works

1. **Initialization**: Start with an initial value x_0.

2. **Function and Hessian Calculation**: In each iteration, evaluate the function and calculate the gradient and Hessian.

3. **Update Variables**: Variables are updated using Newton's rule:

$$x_{\text{new}} = x - H^{-1}\nabla f(x)$$

Where H is the Hessian matrix of the objective function.

4. **Repeat**: This process is repeated until a convergence criterion is met.

Linear Programming

Linear programming is a specific case of optimization where both the objective function and the constraints are linear. It is commonly used in problems of maximization or minimization under linear constraints.

Simplex Method

The simplex method is widely used to solve linear programming problems. It is based on the idea of moving from one optimal vertex to another within the polyhedron that defines the solution until the optima is found.

Example of Linear Programming

Let's use the `scipy.optimize` library in Python to solve a linear programming problem:

```
from scipy.optimize import linprog

```

```
3   # Coefficients of the objective function
4   c = [-5, -3]
        # Coefficients to maximize z = 5x1 + 3x2 (inverted for
        minimization)

5
6   # Coefficients of the constraints
7   A = [[1, 2], [2, 1]]
8   b = [8, 10]
9
10  # Call the optimizer
11  result = linprog(c, A_ub=A, b_ub=b, bounds=(0, None))
12
13  print(f'Status: {result.message}')
14  print(f'Optimal values: x1 = {result.x[0]}, x2 = {result.x[1]
        }')
15  print(f'Optimal value of the objective function: {-result.fun
        }')  # Inverted to show the maximum
```

Applications in Artificial Intelligence

Optimization is crucial in the development of machine learning models and training neural networks. A common example is in the tuning of parameters, where the goal is to minimize error on training data. Methods such as gradient descent and its variants (momentum, Adam, RMSprop) are frequently used.

Example: Training a Neural Network

Neural networks require an optimization process to adjust their weights during training. The objective is to minimize the loss function, which measures the discrepancy between the model's predictions and the actual data. Here, learning is achieved through optimization methods over multiple epochs, updating the network weights to converge the loss function towards its minimum.

Conclusion

Mathematical optimization is an essential field in artificial intelligence that enables the continuous improvement of models and algorithms. From unconstrained optimization to linear programming and advanced methods like Newton's method, each technique presents its unique advantages and challenges. A deep understanding of these methods will create a solid foundation for addressing complex problems in AI, offering researchers and practitioners powerful tools to find optimal solutions in various contexts. As a continuation of this chapter, in the following texts, we will delve deeper into differential calculus and its vital role in model training.

## Chapter 9

Differential Calculus in Model Training

Differential calculus plays an essential role in the field of artificial intelligence (AI), especially in the training of machine learning models. Understanding how differential calculus works is crucial for engineers and researchers seeking to optimize algorithms and develop effective models. This chapter will focus on the fundamental concepts of differential calculus, its importance in model training, and practical examples using Python.

Introduction to Differential Calculus

Differential calculus is a branch of calculus that deals with the study of instantaneous rates of change. It focuses on the derivative, which represents the slope of a function at a given point. In simpler terms, the derivative of a function indicates how the output of that function changes with respect to a change in its input.

The common notation for the derivative is expressed as:

- $f'(x)$ or $\frac{df}{dx}$ for functions of a single variable.

- ∇f for functions of multiple variables (the gradient).

Derivatives are crucial for optimization and the search for minima and maxima in functions, which is essential in AI model training.

Derivatives and Gradient

Derivative

The derivative of a function $f(x)$ is formally defined as the limit of the difference quotient as the increment approaches zero:

$$f'(x) = \lim_{\Delta x \to 0} \frac{f(x+\Delta x)-f(x)}{\Delta x}$$

The derivative has multiple applications. Some of them include:

- **Finding the rate of change of a variable**: For example, if we have a function $f(t)$ that represents the position of a moving object over time, the derivative $f'(t)$ gives us the object's velocity at that moment.

- **Identifying critical points**: These are points where the function may reach a maximum, minimum, or inflection point. For example, when optimizing an AI model, we can use derivatives to locate the parameters that minimize the loss function.

- **Analyzing the concavity of a function**: Through the second derivative, one can determine whether the function is convex or concave, which helps understand whether a local minimum is a global minimum.

Gradient

When working with functions of multiple variables, we utilize the concept of the gradient. The gradient is a vector of partial derivatives that indicates the direction in which the function increases most:

$$\nabla f(x,y) = \left(\frac{\partial f}{\partial x}, \frac{\partial f}{\partial y}\right)$$

The direction of the gradient always points towards the direction of greatest increase of the function. Therefore, to minimize a function, we use the gradient to move in the opposite direction. This notion is fundamental in the gradient descent algorithm, which is an efficient method for finding optima in multivariable functions.

Application of Differential Calculus in AI

In the context of machine learning, differential calculus is primarily used in model training. One of the most common applications is the optimization of the loss function, which measures the discrepancy between the model's predictions and the actual values.

Loss Function

The loss function is fundamental in model training. It is used to quantify how well a model performs given a dataset. It measures the error between the model's predictions and the actual values. Some common loss functions include:

- **Mean Squared Error (MSE)**: Used for regression problems and defined as:

$$MSE = \frac{1}{n} \sum_{i=1}^{n} (y_i - \hat{y}_i)^2$$

where y_i is the actual value and $\hat{y}_i$ is the model's prediction. This function heavily penalizes large errors and is sensitive to outliers.

- **Cross-Entropy**: Used for classification problems and defined as:

$$H(y,\hat{y}) = -\sum_i y_i \log(\hat{y}_i)$$

where y_i is the true class and $\hat{y}_i$ is the predicted probability of the class. Cross-entropy measures how well the predicted probability is distributed relative to the actual distribution, penalizing incorrect predictions.

The loss function is crucial because it defines the objective of learning. Without a function to guide the model on how well it is performing, we could not make adjustments to the parameters. As the loss function is minimized during training, the model's ability to generalize on unseen data is also improved.

Advanced Applications of Differential Calculus

Apart from the basic use of gradient descent, there are different advanced optimization variants that enhance the process and allow for more efficient approaches in training complex models.

Stochastic Gradient Descent (SGD)

Stochastic Gradient Descent (SGD) is a modification of classic gradient descent. Instead of calculating the gradient of the loss function using the entire dataset, each iteration uses only a single example or a small batch (mini-batch) of examples. This makes the learning process less computationally expensive and allows for more frequent updates of the parameters.

Process Description:

1. **Initialization**: The model parameters and the learning rate are set.

2. **Iteration**:

   ○ For each training sample (or batch):

      1. Calculate the predictions.

      2. Calculate the loss function.

      3. Compute the gradient of the loss function with respect to the parameters.

      4. Update the parameters in the opposite direction of the gradient.

3. **Repeat**: This process is repeated for several epochs, during which the data is presented in a manner that ensures randomness.

Example in Python:

```python
import numpy as np

# Generate some dummy data
X = np.random.rand(100, 2)
y = (X[:, 0] + X[:, 1] > 1).astype(int)

# Initialize parameters
weights = np.random.rand(2)
alpha = 0.01  # Learning rate
epochs = 100

# Training using SGD
for epoch in range(epochs):
    for i in range(len(X)):
        x_i = X[i]
        y_i = y[i]
```

```
17
18              # Prediction
19              prediction = 1 / (1 + np.exp(-np.dot(weights, x_i))
     )
20              # Calculate the error
21              error = y_i - prediction
22
23              # Update weights
24              weights += alpha * error * x_i
25
26   print(f'Final weights: {weights}')
```

Adaptive Optimization Methods

Adaptive optimization methods improve gradient descent by adjusting the learning rate based on each parameter. This results in more efficient learning, especially in problems with sparse or noisy characteristics.

Adam (Adaptive Moment Estimation)

Adam is a popular algorithm that combines ideas from two previous methods: the moving average of the gradient (as in RMSprop) and the moving average of the derivatives. The essence of Adam is that it maintains an adaptive average of the gradients as well as the squares of the gradients, allowing the learning rate to be adjusted dynamically.

Process Description:

1. **Initialization**: Initialize first and second order moments (mean and variance).

2. **Iteration**:

- For each parameter:

    1. Calculate the gradients.

    2. Update the moving averages of the first and second moments.

    3. Adjust the learning rate.

    4. Update the parameters.

Example in Python (using TensorFlow or Keras):

```
1  import numpy as np
2  import tensorflow as tf
3
4  # Generate some dummy data
5  X_train = np.random.rand(100, 1)
6  y_train = 2 * X_train + 1 + 0.1 * np.random.randn(100, 1)
   # Linear relationship with noise
7
8  # Create a simple model
9  model = tf.keras.Sequential([tf.keras.layers.Dense(1,
   input_shape=(1,))])
10 model.compile(optimizer='adam', loss='mean_squared_error')
11
12 # Train the model
13 model.fit(X_train, y_train, epochs=100)
```

RMSprop

RMSprop is another adaptive optimization algorithm that maintains an exponentially decaying average of recent squared gradients. This prevents the learning from stagnating during optimization and has been shown to work well in noisy problems.

Process Description:

1. **Initialization**: Initialize a variable to store the average of the squared gradient.

2. **Iteration**:

   ◦ Calculate the gradient.

   ◦ Update the average of the squared gradient.

   ◦ Update the parameters using the adaptive learning rate.

Example in Python (with TensorFlow or Keras):

```python
1   import numpy as np
2   import tensorflow as tf
3
4   # Generate some dummy data for classification
5   X_train = np.random.rand(100, 2)
6   y_train = np.random.randint(0, 2, 100)  # Two classes
7
8   # Create a simple model
9   model = tf.keras.Sequential([
10      tf.keras.layers.Dense(5, activation='relu', input_shape
    =(2,)),
11      tf.keras.layers.Dense(1, activation='sigmoid')
12  ])
13  model.compile(optimizer='rmsprop', loss=
    'binary_crossentropy', metrics=['accuracy'])
14
15  # Train the model
16  model.fit(X_train, y_train, epochs=100)
```

Adagrad

Adagrad is an optimizer that adapts the learning rate based on the frequency of updates for each parameter. If a parameter is updated frequently, its learning rate is reduced, and if it is updated rarely, its learning rate is increased.

Process Description:

1. **Initialization**: Maintain a cumulative average of the squared gradients.

2. **Iteration**:

   ◦ Calculate the gradient.

   ◦ Update the individual learning rate for each parameter.

   ◦ Update the parameters.

Example in Python (with TensorFlow or Keras):

```python
1  import numpy as np
2  import tensorflow as tf
3
4  # Generate some dummy data
5  X_train = np.random.rand(100, 1)
6  y_train = 2 * X_train + 1 + 0.1 * np.random.randn(100, 1)
7
8  # Create a simple model
9  model = tf.keras.Sequential([tf.keras.layers.Dense(1,
     input_shape=(1,))])
10 model.compile(optimizer='adagrad', loss=
     'mean_squared_error')
11
12 # Train the model
```

```
13  model.fit(X_train, y_train, epochs=100)
```

These advanced optimization techniques allow for more efficient training of models in AI and have become standard in the field due to their effectiveness and speed.

Importance of Differential Calculus

Differential calculus is crucial in the development of AI models. Some of its contributions include:

- **Efficient Training**: It enables effective modeling of how changes in parameters affect predictions. This facilitates rapid convergence towards optimal solutions.

- **Advanced Optimization**: It facilitates the implementation of adaptive techniques that are essential for solving complex machine learning problems. These optimizations allow models to fit more accurately to noisy or sparse data, thereby improving their generalization capabilities.

Conclusion

Differential calculus is a powerful tool in artificial intelligence, especially in model training. Understanding how derivatives and gradients work is essential for developing effective optimization algorithms. Throughout this chapter, we have explored the fundamentals of differential calculus and its applications in gradient descent and its variants. This understanding provides a solid foundation for tackling more complex problems in the realm of artificial intelligence and machine learning. In summary, differential calculus not only facilitates continuous improvement in AI models but also enables innovation in techniques and approaches to solve real-world challenges.

## Chapter 10

Numerical Methods for AI

Numerical methods are mathematical techniques designed to solve mathematical problems that cannot be addressed through traditional analytical methods. In the context of artificial intelligence (AI), numerical methods play an essential role, especially in complex problems that require approximate solutions. This chapter will explore different numerical methods applicable to AI, including numerical approximations, the solution of differential equations, and Monte Carlo methods.

Introduction to Numerical Methods

Numerical methods allow the approximation of solutions to mathematical problems by combining mathematical theory and computational power. These methods are used in various fields of science, engineering, and economics, and are fundamental in AI due to their ability to address situations in which exact solutions are difficult or impossible to obtain.

Importance in Artificial Intelligence

In the realm of AI, numerical methods are used in a variety of applications, such as:

- **Model Training**: Many machine learning algorithms require optimization of objective functions that do not have clear analytical solutions.

- **Simulation**: Numerical methods allow the modeling and simulation of complex systems, such as neural networks, with interactions between multiple variables.

- **Solving Differential Equations**: In dynamic models, differential equations are essential for describing the behavior of the system over time.

Numerical Approximations and Their Application

Numerical approximations are techniques that allow for estimating the value of a function or solving equations through methods that do not guarantee exact precision but provide a reasonable approximation. We will examine some of the most common approximations.

Interpolation

Interpolation is a numerical method that estimates the value of a function at a given point based on known values of the function at other points. It is widely used in AI to smooth data or estimate values in datasets where exact data may not be available.

Example of Linear Interpolation

Linear interpolation can be used to estimate intermediate values between two known points. Suppose we know the values of a function at two points (x_0, y_0) and (x_1, y_1). To find the value of y at a new point x, the following formula is used:

$$y = y_0 + \frac{(y_1 - y_0)}{(x_1 - x_0)}(x - x_0)$$

Example in Python:

```python
import numpy as np
import matplotlib.pyplot as plt

# Known data
x_know = np.array([1, 2, 3, 4])
y_know = np.array([1, 4, 9, 16])

# Create a new sample
x_new = np.linspace(1, 4, 10)
y_new = np.interp(x_new, x_know, y_know)

# Visualization
plt.scatter(x_know, y_know, color='red', label=
'Known Points')
plt.plot(x_new, y_new, color='blue', label=
'Linear Interpolation')
plt.title('Linear Interpolation')
plt.xlabel('x')
plt.ylabel('y')
plt.legend()
plt.grid()
```

```
20  plt.show()
```

In this example, known points are used to generate an interpolation and visualize how the interpolator fills in the intermediate values.

Approximations using Taylor Series

Taylor series are another numerical method that uses derivatives to approximate complex functions. A function $f(x)$ can be approximately represented by its Taylor series around a point a:

$$f(x) \approx f(a) + f'(a)(x-a) + \frac{f''(a)}{2!}(x-a)^2 + \cdots + \frac{f^{(n)}(a)}{n!}(x-a)^n$$

This approximation is particularly useful when evaluating nonlinear functions in a programming environment, such as exponential or logarithmic functions.

Example in Python:

```
1  import numpy as np
2  import matplotlib.pyplot as plt
3
4  # Definition of the function and its Taylor series
5  def f(x):
6      return np.exp(x)
7
8  def taylor_series(x, a, n):
9      result = 0
10     for i in range(n + 1):
11         result += (f(a) if i == 0 else np.exp(a) * (x - a)
   ** i / np.math.factorial(i))
```

```
12        return result
13
14   # Data for plotting
15   x_values = np.linspace(-2, 2, 100)
16   y_exact = f(x_values)
17   y_approx = taylor_series(x_values, 0, 4)
     # Taylor approximation of order 4
18
19   # Visualization
20   plt.plot(x_values, y_exact, label='Exact Function: exp(x)',
        color='blue')
21   plt.plot(x_values, y_approx, label='Taylor Approximation',
        color='red', linestyle='--')
22   plt.title('Taylor Approximation')
23   plt.xlabel('x')
24   plt.ylabel('f(x)')
25   plt.legend()
26   plt.grid()
27   plt.show()
```

In this case, the function $\exp(x)$ is estimated around the point $a = 0$ using the Taylor series, comparing it with the actual function to approximate its behavior.

Solving Differential Equations

Differential equations are fundamental in modeling dynamic systems in AI. Many complex phenomena, such as the behavior of neural networks or population dynamics in biology, are described by differential equations. However, these equations often cannot be solved analytically, and numerical methods are employed instead.

Euler's Method

Euler's method is one of the simplest and most effective methods for solving ordinary differential equations (ODEs). This method uses a discrete stepwise approximation to advance the solution of the differential equation.

Description of the Method

Given a differential equation of the form:

$$\frac{dy}{dt} = f(t,y)$$

and a known value $y(t_0)$, Euler's method estimates the value of y at a subsequent step $t_1 = t_0 + h$ as:

$$y(t_1) \approx y(t_0) + h \cdot f(t_0, y(t_0))$$

Example in Python:

```python
import numpy as np
import matplotlib.pyplot as plt

# Definition of the differential equation
def f(t, y):
    return y - t**2 + 1

# Euler method parameters
y0 = 0.5   # Initial condition
t0 = 0     # Initial time
t_final = 2  # Final time
h = 0.1    # Step size
```

```
13
14  # Initialization of the lists for time and solution
15  t_values = np.arange(t0, t_final + h, h)
16  y_values = [y0]
17
18  # Euler method
19  for t in t_values[:-1]:
20      y_new = y_values[-1] + h * f(t, y_values[-1])
21      y_values.append(y_new)
22
23  # Visualization
24  plt.plot(t_values, y_values, marker='o', linestyle='-',
    color='blue')
25  plt.title(
    'Solution of Differential Equation using Euler\'s Method')
26  plt.xlabel('t')
27  plt.ylabel('y(t)')
28  plt.grid()
29  plt.show()
```

In this example, the differential equation is solved using Euler's method to estimate the function over a time range, presenting a satisfactory approximation of the solution.

Other Methods for Differential Equations

In addition to Euler's method, there are more advanced methods that provide improvements in accuracy, such as:

- **Runge-Kutta Methods**: These provide better approximations by calculating several slopes at each step and combining them.

- **Adams-Bashforth Method**: A multi-step method that uses previous evaluations to calculate new values.

Each of these methods applies different strategies to achieve greater accuracy in solving differential equations.

Monte Carlo Methods

Monte Carlo methods are a class of algorithms that rely on random number generation to obtain numerical results. These methods are particularly useful in AI problems that involve high-dimensional integrals, simulations, and optimization.

Basic Concept

The fundamental idea behind Monte Carlo methods is to perform random sampling to estimate the value of a function, integral, or expectation. Any problem that can be framed in probabilistic terms can be addressed through this methodology, making it versatile and powerful.

Integral Estimation

One of the most common uses of Monte Carlo methods is the approximation of definite integrals. Suppose we wish to calculate the integral of a function $f(x)$ between the limits a and b.

The integral can be estimated as:

$$I \approx \frac{b-a}{N} \sum_{i=1}^{N} f(x_i)$$

where N is the total number of samples taken, and each x_i is a randomly generated number uniformly in the interval $[a, b]$.

Example in Python:

```python
1   import numpy as np
2
3   # Definition of the function we want to integrate
4   def f(x):
5       return np.sin(x)
6
7   # Parameters
8   a = 0  # Lower limit
9   b = np.pi  # Upper limit
10  N = 10000  # Number of samples
11
12  # Generating random numbers
13  x_random = np.random.uniform(a, b, N)
14
15  # Approximation of the integral
16  integral_approx = (b - a) / N * np.sum(f(x_random))
17
18  print(f'Approximation of the integral: {integral_approx}')
```

In this code, we use the Monte Carlo method to approximate the integral of the sine function between 0 and π. The precision of the estimation tends to improve as the number of samples N increases.

Applications in AI

In the context of artificial intelligence, Monte Carlo methods can be used in various applications, such as:

- **Stochastic Optimization**: Used in genetic algorithms and reinforcement learning to estimate the expected value of a policy or action.

- **Neural Networks**: In the simulation of deep neural networks, Monte Carlo methods can help address overfitting through the random generation of datasets and bagging techniques.

Conclusion

Numerical methods are fundamental tools in artificial intelligence, enabling the resolution of complex problems in an approximate and efficient manner. From interpolation and function approximation to solving differential equations and using Monte Carlo methods, these methods are applied in various contexts within AI, facilitating the understanding and optimization of models.

As the field of artificial intelligence continues to evolve, understanding these numerical methods and their applications becomes increasingly important for professionals and academics who aspire to develop innovative and effective solutions. In upcoming chapters, we will continue to explore advanced concepts and techniques built upon these essential foundations.

## Chapter 11

Dimensionality Reduction

Dimensionality reduction is a set of techniques used to reduce the number of variables (or dimensions) in a dataset while preserving the most relevant information. In the field of artificial intelligence (AI) and machine learning, dimensionality reduction is fundamental for several reasons, such as simplifying models, improving data visualization, and mitigating overfitting. In this chapter, we will explore the concepts of dimensionality, common techniques for dimensionality reduction, and present practical examples using Python.

Concepts of Dimensionality

When we talk about data, **dimensionality** refers to the number of features or variables that describe each observation. For example, in a dataset about flowers, we might have features such as petal length, petal width, sepal length, and sepal width. Each of these features represents a dimension.

A high-dimensional dataset presents several challenges:

1. **Curse of Dimensionality**: As the number of dimensions increases, the volume of the data space grows exponentially. This means that data points become scattered in an increasingly larger space, making it difficult to capture meaningful relationships among the data. For instance, in a high-dimensional space, points are likely to be farther apart, complicating the task of categorizing or finding patterns.

2. **Computational Costs**: Machine learning algorithms tend to become more expensive in terms of time and resources as the number of dimensions increases.

3. **Overfitting**: In complex models, a high number of dimensions can lead to the model fitting too closely to the training data, capturing noise instead of true patterns. By reducing dimensionality, the model can be simplified and improve its generalization capacity.

Techniques for Dimensionality Reduction

There are several techniques for dimensionality reduction, each suitable for different types of data and objectives. Below, we will focus on two of the most commonly used techniques: Principal Component Analysis (PCA) and Linear Discriminant Analysis (LDA).

Principal Component Analysis (PCA)

Principal Component Analysis (PCA) is a statistical technique that transforms a high-dimensional dataset into a new set of variables, known as principal components, which are orthogonal to each other and ordered in such a way that the first ones retain the most variance present in the original data.

PCA Process

1. **Standardization**: First, the data is standardized to have a mean of zero and a variance of one. This is crucial because PCA relies on variance, and columns with different scales can affect the analysis.

2. **Calculation of the Covariance Matrix**: The covariance matrix is calculated to determine how the different attributes vary together.

3. **Calculation of Eigenvalues and Eigenvectors**: The eigenvalues and eigenvectors of the covariance matrix are obtained. The eigenvalues indicate the amount of variance explained by each of the components.

4. **Selection of Principal Components**: The components are ordered based on their eigenvalues, and the first k components are selected where k is the number of dimensions to retain.

5. **Projection of the Data**: The original data is projected onto the space of the selected components.

PCA Example in Python

```python
1   import numpy as np
2   import pandas as pd
3   import matplotlib.pyplot as plt
4   from sklearn.datasets import load_iris
5   from sklearn.decomposition import PCA
6
7   # Load the Iris dataset
8   iris = load_iris()
9   X = iris.data
10  y = iris.target
```

```
11
12  # Standardization of the data
13  X_std = (X - X.mean(axis=0)) / X.std(axis=0)
14
15  # Apply PCA
16  pca = PCA(n_components=2)
17  X_pca = pca.fit_transform(X_std)
18
19  # Visualize the results
20  plt.figure(figsize=(10, 6))
21  scatter = plt.scatter(X_pca[:, 0], X_pca[:, 1], c=y, cmap=
     'viridis', edgecolor='k')
22  plt.title('Dimensionality Reduction using PCA')
23  plt.xlabel('Principal Component 1')
24  plt.ylabel('Principal Component 2')
25  plt.legend(*scatter.legend_elements(), title='Species')
26  plt.grid()
27  plt.show()
```

In this example, we applied PCA to the Iris dataset, a classic in machine learning. Since the original dataset has four dimensions (lengths and widths of sepals and petals), we reduced this set to two dimensions that can be visually represented.

Linear Discriminant Analysis (LDA)

Linear Discriminant Analysis (LDA) is a supervised technique used not only for dimensionality reduction but also to maximize separation between multiple classes. Unlike PCA, which seeks to maximize global variance in the data, LDA aims to maximize the distance between class means while minimizing variance within each class.

LDA Process

1. **Calculation of Class Means**: We calculate the mean for each class in the dataset.

2. **Calculation of the Covariance Matrix**: We estimate the within-class covariance matrix and the overall covariance matrix.

3. **Calculation of Eigenvalues and Eigenvectors**: Similar to PCA, we find the eigenvalues and eigenvectors of the matrix that results from combining the covariance matrices.

4. **Projection of the Data**: We project the original data into the space generated by the selected eigenvectors.

LDA Example in Python

```python
1  from sklearn.discriminant_analysis import
   LinearDiscriminantAnalysis as LDA
2
3  # Apply LDA
4  lda = LDA(n_components=2)
5  X_lda = lda.fit_transform(X, y)
6
7  # Visualize the results
8  plt.figure(figsize=(10, 6))
9  scatter = plt.scatter(X_lda[:, 0], X_lda[:, 1], c=y, cmap=
   'viridis', edgecolor='k')
10 plt.title('Dimensionality Reduction using LDA')
11 plt.xlabel('Linear Discriminant 1')
12 plt.ylabel('Linear Discriminant 2')
13 plt.legend(*scatter.legend_elements(), title='Species')
14 plt.grid()
```

```
15  plt.show()
```

In this example, we used LDA on the same Iris dataset to project the data into a new space where class separation (flower species) is maximized.

Importance of Dimensionality Reduction

Dimensionality reduction offers several advantages when working with data in AI and machine learning:

1. **Improved Visualization**: It allows for a more intuitive visualization of data, making it easier to identify patterns and relationships.

2. **Reduced Complexity**: By eliminating irrelevant or redundant variables, models are simplified, reducing training time and improving performance.

3. **Prevention of Overfitting**: Dimensionality reduction helps mitigate overfitting by enabling models to generalize better on unseen data.

4. **Reduced Computational Costs**: Fewer dimensions result in lower computational and memory requirements, which can be crucial in production environments.

Final Considerations

While dimensionality reduction is a powerful technique in data analysis, it is essential to use it appropriately. Inappropriate selection of technique or retaining irrelevant dimensions can lead to misleading results. It is crucial to combine dimensionality reduction tactics with a solid understanding of the data and the application in question.

Throughout this chapter, we have explored two of the most popular techniques for dimensionality reduction: PCA and LDA, along with practical examples using Python. This knowledge is just a starting point in the vast realm of dimensionality reduction. As we progress, we can delve deeper into other methods and applications built on these foundations.

## Chapter 12

Feature Spaces in Learning Models

Feature spaces are a fundamental concept in machine learning and artificial intelligence. They refer to the set of attributes (or features) used to describe an object within a model. Understanding how to represent these feature spaces is essential for developing and optimizing effective models, as the choice and transformation of features can significantly impact the quality of predictions. In this chapter, we will explore the representation of data in feature spaces, techniques to improve interpretation and efficiency, and methods for feature selection.

High-Dimensional Data Representation

High-dimensional data representation involves working with parameters that describe data instances across multiple dimensions. For example, in a dataset about flowers, each flower might be represented in a feature space where the dimensions correspond to attributes such as petal length, petal width, sepal length, and sepal width. This approach allows for the creation of models that can learn patterns from the relationships between these features.

The challenges associated with high dimensionality include:

- **Curse of Dimensionality**: As the number of dimensions increases, the distance between data points tends to increase as well. This can make it difficult to identify meaningful relationships among the data and increases the risk of overfitting.

- **Difficulties in Visualization**: Representing data in more than three dimensions becomes complex and often impossible to visualize. This can hinder the interpretation and understanding of relationships within the data.

- **High Computational Costs**: More features require greater processing time and computational resources, which can be a limiting factor in large-scale applications.

Thus, it is vital to identify and represent the most relevant features of the data, optimizing their use in machine learning models.

Improving Interpretation and Efficiency

To enhance the interpretation of a model and its efficiency, it is crucial to apply techniques to transform and optimize the feature space. The most common techniques include normalization, standardization, and creating interactions between features.

Normalization and Standardization

- **Normalization**: This process involves scaling features so that their values lie within a specific range, typically between 0 and 1.

This is achieved using the formula:

$$X' = \frac{X - \min(X)}{\max(X) - \min(X)}$$

Normalization is particularly useful for learning algorithms that use distances, such as K-nearest neighbors (KNN) or neural networks.

- **Standardization**: This technique transforms features so they have a mean of 0 and a standard deviation of 1. The formula used is:

$$X' = \frac{X - \mu}{\sigma}$$

where μ is the mean of the feature and σ is its standard deviation. Standardization is widely used in methods such as linear regression and principal component analysis (PCA).

Example of Normalization and Standardization in Python

```python
1  import numpy as np
2  import pandas as pd
3  from sklearn.preprocessing import MinMaxScaler,
   StandardScaler
4
5  # Creating a sample DataFrame
6  data = {
7      'petal_length': [1.4, 1.3, 1.5, 1.7, 1.5],
8      'petal_width': [0.2, 0.2, 0.4, 0.4, 0.3],
9      'sepal_length': [5.1, 4.9, 5.8, 5.3, 5.5],
10     'sepal_width': [3.5, 3.0, 4.0, 3.1, 3.5]
11  }
12
13  df = pd.DataFrame(data)
14
```

```
15  # Normalization
16  scaler = MinMaxScaler()
17  df_normalized = scaler.fit_transform(df)
18
19  # Standardization
20  scaler = StandardScaler()
21  df_standardized = scaler.fit_transform(df)
22
23  print("Normalized data:\n", df_normalized)
24  print("Standardized data:\n", df_standardized)
```

Creating Interactions Between Features

Sometimes, the relationships between different features can yield additional useful information for the model. Creating interactive features allows for combining two or more original features to form a new feature that can effectively capture certain interactions in the dataset.

For example, if we have features such as height and weight of individuals, creating a new feature called "body mass index" (BMI) that combines both can result in a more effective predictor.

Example of Creating Interactions in Python

```
1  # Creating interactive features
2  df['bmi'] = df['weight'] / (df['height'] ** 2)
       # Assuming height and weight are columns in df
```

Feature Selection Techniques

Feature selection is the process of identifying and retaining only those features that are relevant to the problem at hand. This process not only helps improve model accuracy, but also reduces training time and enhances its generalization capability.

There are several feature selection techniques, which can be categorized into filtering, wrapping, and model-based methods.

Filtering Methods

These methods evaluate the relevance of features independently of the model using statistical metrics. Some common filtering techniques include:

- **Correlation**: Calculating the Pearson correlation coefficient between features and the target variable. Low-correlation features can be eliminated.

- **Statistical Tests**: Using tests such as ANOVA to determine which features have a significant impact on the target variable.

Wrapping Methods

Wrapping methods evaluate feature selection based on the performance of a specific machine learning model. This involves training multiple models with different subsets of features and then comparing their performance. An example of a wrapping technique is backward elimination, which starts with all features and removes the least significant one at each iteration.

Model-Based Methods

These methods use machine learning algorithms to evaluate the importance of features. An example is the use of decision trees, where feature importance is calculated based on how effective each feature has been in improving model accuracy. Models like Random Forest and support vector machines also provide feature importance metrics.

Example of Feature Selection in Python Using Random Forest

```
1  from sklearn.ensemble import RandomForestClassifier
2  import matplotlib.pyplot as plt
3
4
     # Load data (assuming df is our DataFrame and 'target' is
     the target variable)

5  X = df.drop('target', axis=1)
6  y = df['target']
7
8  # Train a Random Forest model
9  model = RandomForestClassifier()
10 model.fit(X, y)
11
12 # Get feature importances
13 importances = model.feature_importances_
14
15 # Visualize importances
16 plt.barh(X.columns, importances)
17 plt.xlabel('Importance')
18 plt.title('Feature Importance')
```

```
19  plt.show()
```

Conclusion

Feature spaces are fundamental in the development of machine learning models. Proper data representation, improved interpretation and efficiency, as well as the application of feature selection techniques, are key aspects that contribute to the effectiveness of a model. Optimizing the feature space not only facilitates model training, but also enables better results in terms of evaluation and generalization.

As we advance in building machine learning models, applying effective transformation and feature selection techniques will be critical to success in solving real-world problems. Proper understanding and manipulation of feature spaces will help us unravel hidden patterns and relationships in the data, leading to more accurate and effective solutions.

## Chapter 13

Game Theory and Its Application in AI

Game theory is an interdisciplinary field that studies strategic interactions among different players, each pursuing their own interests. This theoretical framework is used to understand situations where outcomes depend not only on the decisions made by an individual but also on the decisions made by others. Game theory has found applications in a variety of areas, including economics, biology, politics, and more recently, in artificial intelligence (AI). This chapter focuses on the fundamental elements of game theory, its relevance in AI, and practical examples of applications in competitive algorithms.

Elements of Game Theory

Game theory is based on several key concepts, which are described below:

Players

Players are the agents who make decisions within a game. They can be individuals, groups of individuals (such as companies), or even AI programs. Each player seeks to maximize their own utility or benefit, which can be interpreted as any measure of gain or success in the context of the game.

Strategies

Strategies are the action plans that a player may choose to follow during the game. Depending on the circumstances, a strategy can be simple (e.g., always choosing a specific action) or complex (e.g., varying actions based on the choices of other players).

Payoffs

Payoffs are the rewards or costs that players receive as a result of their decisions. These payoffs are generally represented in the form of a payoff matrix in finite games, where each cell of the matrix shows the outcome for the players given a specific set of strategies.

Types of Games

Games can be classified into different categories, the most relevant being:

- **Simultaneous Games**: Players make their decisions at the same time, without knowing the actions chosen by others. A clear example is the prisoner's dilemma.

- **Sequential Games**: Players make decisions in turns, where each player can observe the actions of previous players. An example would be the game of chess.

- **Cooperative and Non-Cooperative Games**: In cooperative games, players can form coalitions and agree on joint strategies, while in non-cooperative games, each player acts independently.

- **Zero-Sum and Non-Zero-Sum Games**: In a zero-sum game, an increase in one player's payoff means a corresponding decrease in another player's payoff. In contrast, in a non-zero-sum game, it is possible for both players to gain or lose.

Applications of Game Theory in AI

Game theory has influenced the development of modern AI systems, particularly in areas involving interactions among multiple agents. Examples of applications include:

Reinforcement Learning in Multi-Agent Games

Reinforcement learning is a machine learning approach where an agent learns to make decisions through interaction with its environment. In a multi-agent context, each agent must learn not only to maximize its own reward but also to anticipate and adapt to the actions of other agents.

Prisoner's Dilemma

A classic example illustrating multi-agent learning is the prisoner's dilemma. This is commonly presented as follows: two prisoners are arrested and offered a deal: if one betrays the other, the betrayer will be freed while the other receives a long sentence. If both remain silent, they both receive short sentences. If both betray each other, they receive long sentences, but not as long as the one who remains silent. Each prisoner's decision directly affects their outcome, making the prisoner's dilemma a perfect example of a non-cooperative game.

```python
1   import numpy as np
2
3   # Define the payoffs in the prisoner's dilemma
4   def prisoner_payoff(action_a, action_b):
5       # 0: Silent, 1: Betray
6       if action_a == 0 and action_b == 0:
7           return -1, -1   # Both are silent
8       elif action_a == 1 and action_b == 0:
9           return 0, -5    # A betrays B, B is silent
10      elif action_a == 0 and action_b == 1:
11          return -5, 0    # B betrays A, A is silent
12      else:
13          return -3, -3   # Both betray
14
15  # Example of the game
16  actions = [(0, 0), (0, 1), (1, 0), (1, 1)]
17  for action_a, action_b in actions:
18      print(f'Action A: {action_a}, Action B: {action_b}
     -> Payoff: {prisoner_payoff(action_a, action_b)}')
```

Competition and Learning in Competitive Environments

Competition among multiple agents can be modeled using game theory approaches. For example, when developing a content recommendation system, each agent (thematic or product to recommend) can be seen as a player in a game. The success of each agent will depend on how other agents behave in that competitive environment. Here, AI can employ reinforcement learning to adapt its recommendation strategy based on changing user preferences and interactions with other agents.

Negotiation in AI Systems

Negotiation algorithms in AI use principles of game theory to enable multiple agents (like virtual assistants) to negotiate with each other to optimize their resources, such as time, money, or access to information. Through techniques like offer negotiation, agents develop strategies that allow them to reach agreements that benefit all parties involved.

Planning and Strategies in Games

In games like chess or Go, game theory offers a powerful framework for planning strategies. AI algorithms that play chess (like Stockfish) use minimax search techniques combined with heuristics to anticipate possible moves from their opponents. Each move is evaluated not only for its immediate merit but also for its potential impact on the opponent's decisions.

```python
1   import chess
2   import chess.engine
3
4   # Initialize a chess game
5   board = chess.Board()
6
7   # Select a chess engine
8   engine = chess.engine.SimpleEngine.popen_uci(
        "path/to/your/engine")
9
10  # Example of moves
11  while not board.is_game_over():
12      print(board)
13      result = engine.play(board, chess.engine.Limit(time=2.0))
14      board.push(result.move)
15
```

```
16  engine.quit()
```

Final Reflections on Game Theory in AI

Game theory not only provides a framework for understanding complex interactions among multiple agents in artificial intelligence but also offers powerful tools for the design and implementation of competitive algorithms. As we move toward a future where AI is increasingly integrated into collective and collaborative decision-making, the importance of game theory in this context becomes increasingly evident.

Understanding how agents interact and compete for resources is vital for building systems that are not only effective but also ethical and responsible. From this foundation, we will be able to explore more advanced approaches involving game theory and multiple agents in the upcoming chapters.

## Chapter 14

Fundamentals of Matrices for AI Models

Matrices are one of the most commonly used mathematical structures for representing data and manipulating multiple variables simultaneously. In the field of artificial intelligence (AI), the use of matrices is fundamental, as they allow for the representation of data, the execution of complex mathematical operations, and the implementation of efficient algorithms. This chapter focuses on the fundamentals of matrices, their operations, and shows how they can be applied in AI models, illustrated with practical examples.

Introduction to Matrices

A matrix is a rectangular array of numbers organized into rows and columns. The elements of a matrix can be real numbers, complex numbers, or any other type of data that needs to be manipulated. Matrices are often denoted by uppercase letters (e.g., A, B, C).

The dimension of a matrix is described by the number of rows and columns it has, represented as $m \times n$, where m is the number of rows and n is the number of columns. For example, a 2×3 matrix has 2 rows and 3 columns.

Representation of a Matrix

A matrix A of dimension $m \times n$ can be represented as follows:

$$A = \begin{pmatrix} a_{11} & a_{12} & \cdots & a_{1n} \\ a_{21} & a_{22} & \cdots & a_{2n} \\ \vdots & \vdots & \ddots & \vdots \\ a_{m1} & a_{m2} & \cdots & a_{mn} \end{pmatrix}$$

Where a_{ij} represents the element in row i and column j of the matrix.

Matrix Operations

Operations with matrices are fundamental for manipulating and transforming data in AI. Basic operations include:

Matrix Addition

The addition of two matrices A and B of the same dimension is performed by summing the corresponding elements. Addition is defined only if both matrices have the same dimensions.

$$C = A + B \quad \text{where} \quad C_{ij} = A_{ij} + B_{ij}$$

Example:

Suppose we have the following matrices:

$$A = \begin{pmatrix} 1 & 2 \\ 3 & 4 \end{pmatrix}, \quad B = \begin{pmatrix} 5 & 6 \\ 7 & 8 \end{pmatrix}$$

The sum $C = A + B$ would be:

$$C = \begin{pmatrix} 1+5 & 2+6 \\ 3+7 & 4+8 \end{pmatrix} = \begin{pmatrix} 6 & 8 \\ 10 & 12 \end{pmatrix}$$

Matrix Multiplication

The product of matrices is more complex than addition. Two matrices A and B can be multiplied if the number of columns in A is equal to the number of rows in B. If A is of dimension $m \times n$ and B is of dimension $n \times p$, then the result C will be of dimension $m \times p$.

The element C_{ij} is calculated as:

$$C_{ij} = \sum_{k=1}^{n} A_{ik} \cdot B_{kj}$$

Example:

If A and B are the following matrices:

$$A = \begin{pmatrix} 1 & 2 \\ 3 & 4 \end{pmatrix}, \quad B = \begin{pmatrix} 5 & 6 \\ 7 & 8 \end{pmatrix}$$

The product $C = A \cdot B$ is:

$$C = \begin{pmatrix} 1 \cdot 5 + 2 \cdot 7 & 1 \cdot 6 + 2 \cdot 8 \\ 3 \cdot 5 + 4 \cdot 7 & 3 \cdot 6 + 4 \cdot 8 \end{pmatrix} = \begin{pmatrix} 19 & 22 \\ 43 & 50 \end{pmatrix}$$

Transposition

The transpose of a matrix A is denoted as A^T and is obtained by swapping rows for columns. If A is a matrix of dimension $m \times n$, then A^T will have dimension $n \times m$.

Example:

For a matrix A:

$$A = \begin{pmatrix} 1 & 2 \\ 3 & 4 \end{pmatrix}$$

The transpose A^T is:

$$A^T = \begin{pmatrix} 1 & 3 \\ 2 & 4 \end{pmatrix}$$

Determinant and Inverse Matrix

The determinant is a scalar that can be calculated from a square matrix and provides information about the matrix, such as its invertibility. A matrix is invertible if its determinant is different from zero. The inverse matrix A^{-1} is such that:

$$A \cdot A^{-1} = I$$

where I is the identity matrix.

Example:

For the matrix A:

$$A = \begin{pmatrix} 4 & 7 \\ 2 & 6 \end{pmatrix}$$

The determinant $\det(A)$ is calculated as:

$$\det(A) = (4 \cdot 6) - (7 \cdot 2) = 24 - 14 = 10$$

Since the determinant is 10 (not zero), the matrix is invertible. The inverse matrix can be calculated using the formula:

$$A^{-1} = \frac{1}{\det(A)} \begin{pmatrix} d & -b \\ -c & a \end{pmatrix} = \frac{1}{10} \begin{pmatrix} 6 & -7 \\ -2 & 4 \end{pmatrix} = \begin{pmatrix} 0.6 & -0.7 \\ -0.2 & 0.4 \end{pmatrix}$$

Application of Matrices in AI Models

Matrices are fundamental in the development of artificial intelligence models, especially in machine learning and deep learning. Below, we will explore some relevant applications.

Data Representation

In machine learning, data is organized into matrices to facilitate manipulation. For example, in a feature dataset, each row can represent an observation (example) and each column can represent a feature (variable).

```
1   import numpy as np
2
```

```
3   # Example data matrix
4   data = np.array([[5.1, 3.5, 1.4, 0.2],
5                    [4.9, 3.0, 1.4, 0.2],
6                    [4.7, 3.2, 1.3, 0.2],
7                    [4.6, 3.1, 1.5, 0.2]])
8   print("Data Matrix:\n", data)
```

This example shows how a matrix can be constructed to represent characteristics of different observations (in this case, characteristics of Iris flowers).

Prediction Calculation in Models

Machine learning models, such as linear regression or neural networks, use matrix operations to make prediction calculations. In linear regression, for example, the model parameters are represented as a vector, and predictions are obtained through matrix multiplication.

Example of Prediction in Linear Regression

Suppose we have a linear regression model expressed as:

$$y = X \cdot \beta + \diamondsuit$$

where X is the feature matrix, β is the coefficient vector, and $\diamondsuit$ is the error term.

```
1   # Model coefficients
2   beta = np.array([0.5, -0.2, 0.3, 0.1])
3   # Prediction of the observations using the model
4   predictions = np.dot(data, beta)
```

```
5   print("Predictions:\n", predictions)
```

Data Manipulation in Neural Networks

Neural networks use matrices to represent weights and activations between different layers. For example, by multiplying the input matrix by the weight matrix, outputs from the previous layer are obtained, which can then be passed through an activation function.

Example of Output Calculation in a Layer

```
1   # Layer weights
2   weights = np.array([[0.2, 0.4],
3                       [0.5, 0.1],
4                       [0.3, 0.8],
5                       [0.4, 0.7]])
6
7   # Activation of the previous layer
8   activation = np.array([0.6, 1.0, 0.7, 0.5])
9
10  # Calculation of the layer's outputs
11  outputs = np.dot(activation, weights)
12  print("Layer Outputs:\n", outputs)
```

Conclusion

Matrices are fundamental tools in artificial intelligence, especially in the manipulation and representation of data. From basic operations like addition and multiplication to their application in complex machine learning and neural network models, understanding and handling matrices are essential for anyone working in the AI field.

As you advance in understanding more complex topics, the ability to work with matrices becomes an invaluable asset. This chapter has provided a solid foundation on the use of matrices and their operations, which is crucial for the effective development and implementation of artificial intelligence models.

## Chapter 15

Advanced Statistical Models

Statistical models are fundamental tools in data analysis and artificial intelligence (AI), allowing us to interpret and make predictions based on data. As we become familiar with basic statistics, it is crucial to advance towards more complex and sophisticated models that can handle the variety of problems that arise in AI applications. This chapter will focus on some advanced statistical models, including nonlinear models, two-way ANOVA, and more, as well as multivariate analysis. We will not only seek to understand the theory behind these models but also how they are applied in real-world situations, using practical examples in Python.

Introduction to Nonlinear Models

Nonlinear models are those in which the relationship between the dependent variable and the independent variables cannot be adequately described by a straight line. Nonlinear modeling is valuable when the data exhibit complex patterns that cannot be captured by simple linear models.

Common types of nonlinear models include:

- **Polynomial regression models**: Relationships that can be described by polynomials of degree two or higher.

- **Exponential models**: Used to describe phenomena that grow or decay at rates proportional to their size.

- **Logarithmic models**: Describe the relationship between variables on a logarithmic scale.

- **Diffusion models**: Employed in social sciences to model phenomena such as the diffusion of innovations in a population.

For example, consider a case where one wants to model the growth of a bacterial population. A simple model might be linear, but in practice, the growth of bacteria resembles an exponential model until resource limits are reached.

Example of Nonlinear Regression

We can visualize an example of polynomial regression using Python. Assuming we have a dataset that describes the growth of a bacterial population over time.

```python
import numpy as np
import matplotlib.pyplot as plt
from sklearn.preprocessing import PolynomialFeatures
from sklearn.linear_model import LinearRegression

# Sample data
time = np.array([0, 1, 2, 3, 4, 5])
population = np.array([1, 2.5, 4.5, 8, 14, 20])
# Nonlinear growth

# Reshape time into a matrix
time_reshaped = time.reshape(-1, 1)
```

```
12
13  # Create a polynomial model of degree 2
14  poly_model = PolynomialFeatures(degree=2)
15  time_poly = poly_model.fit_transform(time_reshaped)
16
17  # Fit linear regression to the polynomial model
18  regression_model = LinearRegression()
19  regression_model.fit(time_poly, population)
20
21  # Predictions
22  predicted_population = regression_model.predict(time_poly)
23
24  # Visualization
25  plt.scatter(time, population, color='red', label=
    'Actual Data')
26  plt.plot(time, predicted_population, label=
    'Polynomial Model', color='blue')
27  plt.title('Polynomial Regression')
28  plt.xlabel('Time')
29  plt.ylabel('Population')
30  plt.legend()
31  plt.grid()
32  plt.show()
```

In this example, we fit a polynomial model of degree 2 to the population and time data, visualizing how the curve fits the nonlinear growth data.

Two-Way ANOVA

Analysis of Variance (ANOVA) is a statistical technique used to compare the means of different groups and determine if there are significant differences between them. Two-way ANOVA extends this analysis by allowing the comparison of group means based on two independent variables.

Context of Two-Way ANOVA

Contexts where two-way ANOVA is applied include experimental studies where the interaction of two different factors and their effects on a dependent variable are to be understood. For example, imagine an experiment designed to analyze how different types of fertilizers (Factor A) and watering levels (Factor B) affect plant growth.

Since we are interested in seeing if there are interactions between the two variables regarding growth, we apply two-way ANOVA.

Practical Example of Two-Way ANOVA

First, we would need a dataset, which might look like this:

Fertilizer	Low Watering	High Watering
A	22	30
A	24	31
B	20	28
B	19	29
C	25	36
C	27	34

Using Python and the `statsmodels` library, we can perform a two-way ANOVA.

```
1  import pandas as pd
2  import statsmodels.api as sm
3  from statsmodels.formula.api import ols
4  from statsmodels.stats.anova import anova_lm
5
6  # Create the DataFrame
```

```
7   data = {
8       'Fertilizer': ['A', 'A', 'B', 'B', 'C', 'C', 'A', 'A',
    'B', 'B', 'C', 'C'],
9       'Watering': ['Low', 'High', 'Low', 'High', 'Low',
    'High', 'Low', 'High', 'Low', 'High', 'Low', 'High'],
10      'Growth': [22, 30, 20, 28, 25, 36, 24, 31, 19, 29, 27,
    34]
11  }
12
13  df = pd.DataFrame(data)
14
15  # Two-Way ANOVA Model
16  model = ols(
    'Growth ~ C(Fertilizer) + C(Watering) +
    C(Fertilizer):C(Watering)'
    , data=df).fit()
17  anova_results = anova_lm(model)
18
19  print(anova_results)
```

This code generates results that show if there are significant interactions and how each factor influences growth.

Multivariate Analysis

Multivariate analysis refers to a set of statistical techniques used to analyze more than one variable at the same time. It is especially useful when understanding complex interrelationships among multiple variables is required, such as in market research, biology, or social sciences.

Common multivariate analysis techniques include:

- **Principal Component Analysis (PCA)**: Used to reduce the dimensionality of the data while preserving most of the original variation.

- **Discriminant Analysis**: Aims to find a combination of features that best distinguishes between classes.

Example of Multivariate Analysis with PCA

Consider an iris dataset where we want to reduce dimensions for 2D visualization. We will use the `sklearn` library for this purpose.

```python
from sklearn.datasets import load_iris
from sklearn.decomposition import PCA

# Load the iris dataset
iris = load_iris()
X = iris.data

# PCA
pca = PCA(n_components=2)
X_reduced = pca.fit_transform(X)

# Visualization
plt.figure(figsize=(8, 6))
plt.scatter(X_reduced[:, 0], X_reduced[:, 1], c=iris.target
, cmap='viridis')
plt.title(
'Principal Component Analysis (PCA) on the Iris Dataset')
plt.xlabel('Principal Component 1')
plt.ylabel('Principal Component 2')
plt.colorbar(ticks=[0, 1, 2], label='Species')
plt.grid()
plt.show()
```

This code applies PCA to the iris dataset, reducing dimensions and allowing a clearer visualization of how the species group based on measured characteristics.

Conclusions

Advanced statistical models are fundamentally important in the fields of artificial intelligence and data analysis. From understanding nonlinear relationships to employing sophisticated techniques such as two-way ANOVA and multivariate analysis, statistics enhances our ability to make data-driven decisions.

A solid understanding of these models allows AI professionals to develop more informed approaches to dealing with complex datasets, thereby enabling deeper analyses and more accurate predictions. As one continues to learn and explore the rich intersection between statistics and artificial intelligence, new opportunities will arise to innovate in the realm of data analysis and predictive modeling.

## Chapter 16

Stochastic Simulation and Modeling

Stochastic simulation and modeling are essential tools in data analysis and artificial intelligence (AI). As we try to understand and predict complex systems across multiple fields, from economics to biology, the need for methods that can handle uncertainty and variability becomes evident. In this chapter, we will explore the concepts of simulation and stochastic modeling, their importance in AI, and practical examples of their implementation using Python.

Importance of Simulation in AI

Simulation is the process of creating a model that represents a real system and then conducting experiments on that model to understand its behavior. This approach is particularly valuable in situations where the real system is costly, dangerous, or simply impossible to experiment with in practice. For example, simulating traffic in a city to study the impact of new routes or changes in signage before physically implementing them.

Simulation is also used to generate data, which is fundamental in training AI models, especially when there is not enough real data available. Through simulation, scenarios can be generated that allow models to learn about different conditions and behaviors.

Moreover, simulation enables the analysis of variability in outcomes and assesses how different factors influence the system's results.

Stochastic Modeling

On the other hand, stochastic modeling refers to the construction of models that incorporate randomness. Unlike deterministic models, which assume that the outcome of a process is fixed and predictable, stochastic models consider that outcomes vary due to the inherent uncertainty in the systems being studied.

In basic terms, a stochastic model can be thought of as a series of random experiments. For example, when modeling the waiting time in a customer service queue, we can assume that the arrival time of customers follows a probabilistic distribution. This implies that, while we can calculate an average, each customer has an arrival time that may deviate from this mean.

Common Simulation Techniques

There are several simulation techniques that have been widely used in AI and data analysis. Below, we will explore the most common ones:

Monte Carlo

The Monte Carlo method is a simulation technique that uses randomness to solve problems that can be deterministic in principle. It relies on repeating random simulations to obtain results that represent the general behavior of the system under study. This method is applicable in fields such as optimization, finance, and physics, and is particularly useful for evaluating complex integrals.

Monte Carlo Simulation Example

Suppose we want to estimate the value of π using the Monte Carlo method. The idea is to generate random points within a square that circumscribes a quarter circle and count how many of those points fall inside the circle.

```python
1   import numpy as np
2   import matplotlib.pyplot as plt
3
4   # Number of points to generate
5   n = 10000
6   # Generate random points
7   x = np.random.rand(n)
8   y = np.random.rand(n)
9
10  # Calculate how many points fall inside the quarter circle
11  inside_circle = (x**2 + y**2) <= 1
12
13  # Estimate π
14  pi_estimate = 4 * np.sum(inside_circle) / n
15  print(f'estimation of π: {pi_estimate}')
16
17  # Visualize
```

```
18  plt.figure(figsize=(8, 8))
19  plt.scatter(x[inside_circle], y[inside_circle], color=
    'blue', s=1, label='Inside the circle')
20  plt.scatter(x[~inside_circle], y[~inside_circle], color=
    'red', s=1, label='Outside the circle')
21  plt.legend()
22  plt.title('Estimation of π using the Monte Carlo Method')
23  plt.xlabel('X')
24  plt.ylabel('Y')
25  plt.axis('equal')
26  plt.grid()
27  plt.show()
```

In this code, we generate 10,000 random points and calculate how many fell inside the quarter circle. The estimation of π is obtained from the ratio of the number of points inside the circle to the total number of points generated.

Discrete Event Simulation

Discrete event simulation is another common technique that is used to model systems where unique events occur at specific times. A typical example is the queueing system, where customers arrive at a service point and wait their turn.

This type of simulation allows modeling the behavior of the system based on arrival and service rates and is useful in applications such as operations management, logistics, and services.

Discrete Event Simulation Example

Let's look at a simple example of how we can model a queueing system using Python. We will assume that customers arrive at a service counter following a Poisson process.

```python
import numpy as np
import matplotlib.pyplot as plt

# Parameters
num_clients = 100
arrival_lambda = 1.0  # arrival rate
service_lambda = 2.0   # service rate

# Customer arrivals (inter-arrival times)
arrival_times = np.cumsum(np.random.exponential(1 /
  arrival_lambda, num_clients))
# Service times
service_times = np.random.exponential(1 / service_lambda,
  num_clients)

# Simulation of start and end service times
start_times = np.zeros(num_clients)
end_times = np.zeros(num_clients)

for i in range(num_clients):
    if i == 0:
        start_times[i] = arrival_times[i]
    else:
        start_times[i] = max(arrival_times[i], end_times[i-
1])
    end_times[i] = start_times[i] + service_times[i]

# Plot results
plt.figure(figsize=(12, 6))
plt.step(arrival_times, np.arange(1, num_clients + 1),
  label="Arrivals", where='post', color='blue')
plt.step(start_times, np.arange(1, num_clients + 1), label=
  "Start of Service", where='post', color='orange')
```

```
29  plt.step(end_times, np.arange(1, num_clients + 1), label=
    "End of Service", where='post', color='green')
30  plt.title('Discrete Event Simulation in a Queueing System')
31  plt.xlabel('Time')
32  plt.ylabel('Number of Clients')
33  plt.legend()
34  plt.grid()
35  plt.show()
```

In this example, we simulated the arrivals and service times of 100 clients. The arrival times are generated using an exponential distribution, and then we determine when each client starts and finishes their service. The visualization helps to understand how the system behaves over time.

Agent-Based Models

Another simulation technique is agent-based modeling, which is used to model complex systems where interactions among individual agents (which can represent people, companies, animals, etc.) give rise to emergent behaviors in the system. This approach is useful in fields such as sociology, economics, and epidemiology.

Agent-based modeling allows simulating scenarios involving decisions, learning, and agents' adaptations to their environment.

Agent-Based Modeling Example

Suppose we want to model the spread of a disease in a population. Each agent in our model represents an individual who can be healthy, infected, or recovered.

```python
1   import matplotlib.pyplot as plt
2   import random
3
4   # Model parameters
5   num_agents = 100
6   initial_infected = 5
7   steps = 50
8
9   # States: 0 = healthy, 1 = infected, 2 = recovered
10  agents = [0] * num_agents
11  infected_indices = random.sample(range(num_agents),
    initial_infected)
12  for i in infected_indices:
13      agents[i] = 1
14
15  # Simulation
16  history = [agents.copy()]
17
18  for _ in range(steps):
19      for i in range(num_agents):
20          if agents[i] == 1:  # If the agent is infected
21              # Infect other agents
22              for j in range(num_agents):
23                  if agents[j] == 0 and random.random() < 0.1
    :  # Probability of contagion
24                      agents[j] = 1  # Infect
25              agents[i] = 2  # The agent recovers
26
27      history.append(agents.copy())
28
29  # Visualization of the spread
30  plt.figure(figsize=(10, 6))
31  total_infected = [sum(1 for agent in step if agent == 1)
    for step in history]
32  plt.plot(total_infected, label='Infected')
```

```
33  plt.xlabel('Steps')
34  plt.ylabel('Number of Infected')
35  plt.title('Agent-Based Model: Disease Spread')
36  plt.legend()
37  plt.grid()
38  plt.show()
```

In this example, we simulate the spread of a disease in a population of agents. Each agent has the possibility to infect others, highlighting how interactions between individual agents can lead to collective patterns.

Conclusions

Simulation and stochastic modeling are fundamental for managing uncertainty and complexity in real systems. From estimating π using the Monte Carlo method to discrete event simulation in queueing systems and agent-based modeling, these techniques provide powerful tools to build models that can help understand and predict complex phenomena.

The use of simulation in artificial intelligence is varied and will extend to multiple applications, from data generation to scenario exploration, all while seeking to optimize and improve decision-making. With the ongoing development of simulation and stochastic modeling techniques, the ability of AI systems to tackle new challenges will expand, offering more robust and versatile solutions to real-world problems.

## Chapter 17

Delving into Probability Theory

Probability theory is a fundamental branch of mathematics that deals with the analysis of random phenomena. In the context of artificial intelligence (AI), this theory is essential, as many algorithms and models rely on the understanding of probability and statistics. In this chapter, we will delve into critical concepts of probability theory, such as Markov models and the central limit theorem. Through examples, illustrations, and Python code, we will seek to provide a solid understanding of how these concepts apply in the field of AI.

Introduction to Probability Theory

Probability measures the certainty of an event occurring. It is numerically represented on a scale from 0 to 1, where 0 indicates that the event will not occur, and 1 indicates that the event will occur with certainty. Events can be simple (single occurrences, like rolling a die) or compound (combinations of events). The sum of the probabilities of all events in a sample space must equal 1.

Sample Space and Events

The **sample space** is the set of all possible outcomes of a random experiment. For example, when rolling a die, the sample space can be represented as:

$$S = \{1, 2, 3, 4, 5, 6\}$$

An **event** is a subset of this space. For example, the event of rolling an even number can be expressed as:

$$E = \{2, 4, 6\}$$

The **probability** of an event E is calculated as:

$$P(E) = \frac{\text{Number of favorable outcomes}}{\text{Total number of possible outcomes}} = \frac{3}{6} = 0.5$$

Markov Models

Markov models are fundamental in probability theory and are used to model systems that evolve over time. The distinguishing characteristic of a Markov model is that the future state of the system depends only on the current state and not on past states. This property is known as the **Markov property**.

Markov Chains

A **Markov chain** is a sequence of states where the probability of transitioning to a new state depends solely on the current state. A common way to represent a Markov chain is through a **transition matrix**.

Example of a Markov Chain

Suppose we are modeling the weather in a city, where the states are "Sunny," "Cloudy," and "Rainy." The transition matrix that describes the weather behavior could be as follows:

$$P = \begin{pmatrix} 0.8 & 0.1 & 0.1 \\ 0.3 & 0.4 & 0.3 \\ 0.2 & 0.5 & 0.3 \end{pmatrix}$$

This matrix means that if today is sunny, there is an 80% chance that tomorrow will also be sunny, a 10% chance that it will be cloudy, and a 10% chance that it will rain. Let's analyze this model with an example in Python.

```python
1  import numpy as np
2
3  # Definition of the transition matrix
4  P = np.array([[0.8, 0.1, 0.1],
5                [0.3, 0.4, 0.3],
6                [0.2, 0.5, 0.3]])
7
8  # States: 0 = Sunny, 1 = Cloudy, 2 = Rainy
9  states = ["Sunny", "Cloudy", "Rainy"]
10
11 # Initial State
12 current_state = 0  # Sunny
13 number_of_days = 10
14 history = [current_state]
15
16 for _ in range(number_of_days):
17     current_state = np.random.choice([0, 1, 2], p=P[
   current_state])
```

```
18        history.append(current_state)
19
20    # Show the history of states
21    weather_history = [states[i] for i in history]
22    print("Weather History:", weather_history)
```

This code simulates the states of the weather over 10 days based on the defined transition matrix. The result will be a sequence of days in which the weather changes according to the probabilities specified in the matrix.

Central Limit Theorem

The **central limit theorem** is one of the most important results in probability theory. It states that, given a sufficiently large number of independent and identically distributed observations (iid), the mean of those observations will be normally distributed, regardless of the original distribution of the population from which they come.

This has significant implications in statistics and artificial intelligence, as it allows for inferences about populations based on small samples and makes statistical methods effective even when the data do not come from a normal distribution.

Example of the Central Limit Theorem

Suppose we want to see how the mean of a sample of data from a uniform distribution behaves as we increase the sample size. Let's simulate this with Python.

```
1    import matplotlib.pyplot as plt
2
```

```python
3  # Definition of parameters
4  n_samples = 1000
5  sample_size = [5, 10, 30, 100]  # Different sample sizes
6  means = []
7
8  # Simulation
9  for n in sample_size:
10     sample_means = [np.mean(np.random.uniform(0, 10, n))
   for _ in range(n_samples)]
11     means.append(sample_means)
12
13 # Visualization of results
14 plt.figure(figsize=(12, 8))
15 for i, n in enumerate(sample_size):
16     plt.hist(means[i], bins=30, alpha=0.5, label=
   f'Sample Size: {n}', density=True)
17
18 plt.title('Central Limit Theorem')
19 plt.xlabel('Sample Mean')
20 plt.ylabel('Probability Density')
21 plt.legend()
22 plt.grid()
23 plt.show()
```

In this example, we generate 1000 samples of different sizes and calculate their means. By plotting the histograms of the means, we can observe how, as the sample size increases, the distribution of the means approaches a normal distribution, illustrating the central limit theorem.

Applications in AI

Probability theory, through concepts like Markov chains and the central limit theorem, has multiple applications in artificial intelligence:

1. **Sequence Modeling**: Markov chains are used in text generation models and time series analysis, where the probability of the next word or element depends on the previous ones.

2. **Machine Learning Algorithms**: Probabilistic models, such as mixture models and Bayesian models, use principles of probability to make inferences and predictions based on data.

3. **Uncertainty Assessment**: Understanding probabilities enables models to manage uncertainty in decision-making, helping systems adapt and respond to changing environments.

Conclusion

Delving into probability theory, especially through concepts like Markov models and the central limit theorem, provides a solid foundation for understanding how many algorithms and inferences in artificial intelligence work. Probability allows us to model the inherent uncertainty in data and make predictions based on observed patterns.

As we advance in exploring more advanced topics in applied mathematics to AI, the understanding of probability theory will remain an invaluable tool in our analytical toolbox.

## Chapter 18

Advanced Regression Models

Regression is a fundamental statistical tool used to model and analyze the relationship between a dependent variable and one or more independent variables. While linear regression is a basic starting point, there are multiple advanced models that allow for handling more complex relationships and addressing different modeling problems. In this chapter, we will explore advanced regression models, including Ridge regression, Lasso regression, and Support Vector Machine (SVM) models. We will also discuss how to choose the right model and evaluate its performance.

Introduction to Advanced Regression

Advanced regression is primarily used in scenarios where the data exhibits characteristics that cannot be adequately described by a simple straight line. These may include:

- High dimensionality: Where the number of features is greater than the number of observations.

- Multicollinearity: When the independent variables are highly correlated with each other.

- Complex interactions: Where the relationships between variables are nonlinear or involve interactions among several variables.

Each of these issues can lead to inefficient, overfitted, or poorly generalized models. Below, we will explore how advanced regression models address these challenges.

Ridge Regression

Ridge regression is a type of linear regression that employs regularization techniques to mitigate the problem of overfitting, particularly in high-dimensional scenarios. This is achieved by introducing a penalty term on the coefficients of the variables in the regression cost function.

Ridge Regression Formula

The goal of ridge regression is to minimize the following cost function:

$$J(\beta) = \sum_{i=1}^{n}(y_i - \hat{y}_i)^2 + \lambda \sum_{j=1}^{p} \beta_j^2$$

Where:

- y_i are the observed values.

- $\hat{y}_i$ are the predicted values.

- β_j are the regression coefficients.

- λ is the regularization parameter that determines the amount of penalty.

By introducing this penalty term λ, Ridge regression helps to reduce the magnitude of the coefficients, which can be beneficial in cases where multicollinearity exists among the features.

Implementation in Python

Let's see how to implement Ridge regression using the `scikit-learn` library.

```python
1   import numpy as np
2   import pandas as pd
3   from sklearn.model_selection import train_test_split
4   from sklearn.linear_model import Ridge
5   from sklearn.metrics import mean_squared_error
6
7   # Generate a simulated dataset
8   np.random.seed(0)
9   X = np.random.rand(100, 10)
    # 100 observations, 10 features
10  true_coefficients = np.array([1.5, -2.0, 3.0] + [0]*7)
    # True coefficients
11  y = X @ true_coefficients + np.random.normal(0, 0.5, size=
    100)  # Generate the dependent variable
12
13  # Split the dataset into training and testing sets
14  X_train, X_test, y_train, y_test = train_test_split(X, y,
     test_size=0.2, random_state=42)
15
16  # Create a Ridge regression model
17  ridge_model = Ridge(alpha=1.0)  # Penalty parameter
18  ridge_model.fit(X_train, y_train)
19
20  # Predict and evaluate
21  y_pred = ridge_model.predict(X_test)
22  mse = mean_squared_error(y_test, y_pred)
23
```

```
24  print(f"Ridge Regression MSE: {mse}")
25  print("Coefficients:", ridge_model.coef_)
```

In this code, we first generate a simulated dataset with 100 observations and 10 features. Then, a Ridge regression model is fitted and evaluated using the mean squared error (MSE) as a performance measure.

Lasso Regression

Lasso regression (Least Absolute Shrinkage and Selection Operator) is another regularization technique that, like Ridge regression, seeks to prevent overfitting. However, instead of applying a penalty to the square of the coefficients, it uses the sum of the absolute values of the coefficients. This can lead to some coefficients being exactly zero, allowing for variable selection.

Lasso Regression Formula

The cost function for Lasso regression is:

$$J(\beta) = \sum_{i=1}^{n}(y_i - \hat{y}_i)^2 + \lambda \sum_{j=1}^{p} |\beta_j|$$

Here, the penalty λ controls the complexity of the model and, like in ridge regression, provides a neat balance between fitting and simplicity.

Implementation in Python

Let's implement Lasso regression on the same simulated dataset.

```
1  from sklearn.linear_model import Lasso
```

```
 2
 3  # Create a Lasso regression model
 4  lasso_model = Lasso(alpha=0.1)  # Penalty parameter
 5  lasso_model.fit(X_train, y_train)
 6
 7  # Predict and evaluate
 8  y_pred_lasso = lasso_model.predict(X_test)
 9  mse_lasso = mean_squared_error(y_test, y_pred_lasso)
10
11  print(f"Lasso Regression MSE: {mse_lasso}")
12  print("Lasso Coefficients:", lasso_model.coef_)
```

In this snippet of code, a Lasso regression model is fitted and the results are evaluated, observing how many coefficients become exactly zero due to the Lasso penalty.

Support Vector Machines (SVM)

Support Vector Machines (SVM) are another popular approach in regression and classification. Originally designed for classification, SVMs can also be adapted for regression through a version called **Support Vector Regression (SVR)**.

The idea behind SVM is to find a hyperplane that separates the classes of data while maximizing the margin between classes. For regression, the goal is to predict a value while minimizing error.

Implementation of Support Vector Regression

In a regression context, SVR uses the points closest to the fitting line (called support vectors) and provides a margin in which the error is considered acceptable.

Next, we will implement SVR in Python.

```
1   from sklearn.svm import SVR
2
3   # Create an SVR model
4   svr_model = SVR(kernel='rbf', C=100, gamma=0.1, epsilon=0.1)
5   svr_model.fit(X_train, y_train)
6
7   # Predict and evaluate
8   y_pred_svr = svr_model.predict(X_test)
9   mse_svr = mean_squared_error(y_test, y_pred_svr)
10
11  print(f"SVR MSE: {mse_svr}")
```

In this code, an SVR model is fitted using the radial basis function (RBF) kernel, which is suitable for modeling nonlinear relationships.

Choosing the Right Model

The choice of the appropriate regression model depends on several factors, including the nature of the data, dimensionality, multicollinearity, and relationships among variables. Some general guidelines are:

1. **Evaluate Multicollinearity**: If there is high correlation among variables, consider regularization methods like Ridge or Lasso.

2. **Feature Selection**: If variable reduction is desired, Lasso regression is preferable due to its ability to set coefficients to zero.

3. **Nonlinearity**: If nonlinear relationships are suspected, SVMs are a robust option.

4. **Model Interpretability**: If interpretability is crucial, Ridge or Lasso regression models may be preferred, although SVM offers less

transparency regarding its internal workings.

Model Performance Evaluation

Evaluating the performance of a regression model is essential for determining its effectiveness. Common metrics for regression include:

- **Mean Squared Error (MSE)**: Provides a measure of the magnitude of the squared error between predictions and actual values.

- **Root Mean Squared Error (RMSE)**: The square root of the MSE, which has the same units as the dependent variable.

- **R^2 (Coefficient of Determination)**: A measure that indicates the proportion of variance in the dependent variable that is predictable from the independent variables.

```
from sklearn.metrics import r2_score

r2_ridge = r2_score(y_test, y_pred)
r2_lasso = r2_score(y_test, y_pred_lasso)
r2_svr = r2_score(y_test, y_pred_svr)

print(f"R² of Ridge Regression: {r2_ridge}")
print(f"R² of Lasso Regression: {r2_lasso}")
print(f"R² of SVR: {r2_svr}")
```

Conclusion

Advanced regression models, including Ridge regression, Lasso regression, and Support Vector Machines, provide powerful tools for modeling complex relationships in data. Understanding how and when to apply each model is crucial for obtaining meaningful results and enhancing predictive capability.

As one advances in the understanding and application of these methods, it becomes evident that the choice of the model and the evaluation of its performance are fundamental elements for success in the fields of machine learning and artificial intelligence. Continuous practice and experimentation will enable professionals to refine their skills in effectively applying these models.

## Chapter 19

Inference and Parameter Estimation

Statistical inference is one of the most powerful branches of statistics, serving as the fundamental heart of many methods used in artificial intelligence and machine learning. This chapter will focus on exploring the concepts of inference and parameter estimation, emphasizing maximum likelihood estimation and the construction of confidence intervals. We will illustrate the concepts with practical examples in Python, aiming to provide a clear and applicable understanding of these methodologies.

Introduction to Statistical Inference

Statistical inference involves using sample data to make claims or draw conclusions about a larger population. This type of inference is crucial in AI, as it typically works with datasets that are only samples of broader populations.

There are two main types of inference:

1. **Estimation Inference**: Refers to the approximation of unknown population parameters using statistics calculated from a sample.

2. **Hypothesis Inference**: Involves making claims about a specific parameter (generally under a null hypothesis) and using statistical tests to determine if there is enough evidence to reject that hypothesis.

Statistical inference seeks to answer questions such as: "What is the mean of a population based on the sample mean?" or "Are there significant differences between two groups?"

Parameter Estimation

Parameter estimation refers to the process of approximating unknown characteristics of a population. This is typically done using statistics calculated from the sample.

Estimators

An **estimator** is a rule or formula used to calculate an estimate of a population parameter. There are two main types of estimators:

- **Point Estimators**: Provide a single value as the best approximation for the population parameter. For example, the sample mean is a point estimator of the population mean.

- **Interval Estimators**: Provide a range of values within which the population parameter is expected to fall. This is done using **confidence intervals**.

Maximum Likelihood Estimation

Maximum likelihood estimation (MLE) is a widely used method for finding the parameters of a statistical model. It involves choosing the parameters that maximize the probability of observing the given data under the model.

How Does It Work?

Suppose we have a dataset $X = \{x_1, x_2, \ldots, x_n\}$ that is assumed to come from a distribution with an unknown parameter θ. The likelihood function $L(\theta)$ is defined as the product of the density (or probability) functions of each observation:

$$L(\theta) = \prod_{i=1}^{n} f(x_i \mid \theta)$$

Where f is the density or probability function of the model. Maximum likelihood estimation involves finding θ that maximizes $L(\theta)$.

Often, it is easier to work with the logarithm of the likelihood function, known as **log-likelihood**:

$$\ell(\theta) = \log(L(\theta)) = \sum_{i=1}^{n} \log(f(x_i \mid \theta))$$

Practical Example of MLE

Suppose we have a dataset that is normally distributed and we want to estimate the mean μ and variance σ^2 of the population. The density function of a normally distributed random variable is expressed as:

$$f(x \mid \mu, \sigma^2) = \frac{1}{\sqrt{2\pi\sigma^2}} e^{-\frac{(x-\mu)^2}{2\sigma^2}}$$

In this case, the log-likelihood becomes:

$$\ell(\mu, \sigma^2) = -\frac{n}{2}\log(2\pi) - \frac{n}{2}\log(\sigma^2) - \frac{1}{2\sigma^2}\sum_{i=1}^{n}(x_i - \mu)^2$$

In this scenario, formulas for μ and σ^2 can be derived:

1. The maximum likelihood estimate for the mean is the sample mean:

$$\hat{\mu} = \frac{1}{n}\sum_{i=1}^{n}x_i$$

2. The maximum likelihood estimate for the variance is:

$$\hat{\sigma}^2 = \frac{1}{n}\sum_{i=1}^{n}(x_i - \hat{\mu})^2$$

Now let's implement this in Python:

```python
import numpy as np

# Generate a simulated dataset
np.random.seed(42)
data = np.random.normal(loc=5, scale=2, size=1000)
    # Mean = 5, Standard deviation = 2

# Maximum likelihood estimates
mu_hat = np.mean(data)
sigma_hat_squared = np.var(data, ddof=0)
    # Use ddof=0 for MLE

print(f"MLE estimate for the mean (mu): {mu_hat}")
print(f"MLE estimate for the variance (sigma^2): {
    sigma_hat_squared}")
```

In this example, we generated a dataset that follows a normal distribution and calculated the maximum likelihood estimates for the mean and variance using Python.

Construction of Confidence Intervals

A **confidence interval** (CI) is a range of values derived from the sample that is likely to contain the value of the considered population parameter. A CI is characterized by a confidence level, typically expressed as a percentage (e.g., 95%).

Interpretation of a Confidence Interval

If a 95% confidence interval is estimated for the mean of a population, it means that if multiple samples were taken and confidence intervals were calculated for each, approximately 95% of those intervals would contain the true value of the population mean.

Calculating the Confidence Interval for the Mean

Suppose we are working with a sample of size n, with a sample mean $\bar{x}$ and a sample standard deviation s. The confidence interval for the population mean is calculated as:

$$CI = \bar{x} \pm z_{\alpha/2} \frac{s}{\sqrt{n}}$$

Where $z_{\alpha/2}$ is the critical z-value corresponding to the desired confidence level. For a 95% CI, $z_{\alpha/2} \approx 1.96$.

Practical Example of Constructing a Confidence Interval

Using the dataset from the previous example, let's calculate a 95% confidence interval for the population mean.

```
1   import scipy.stats as stats
2
3   # Parameters
4   n = len(data)
5   alpha = 0.05  # Significance level
6   z_critical = stats.norm.ppf(1 - alpha/2)  # Critical z-value
7
8   # Sample mean and standard deviation
9   mean_sample = np.mean(data)
10  std_sample = np.std(data, ddof=1)
        # ddof=1 for sample standard deviation calculation
11
12  # Calculate the margin of error
13  margin_of_error = z_critical * (std_sample / np.sqrt(n))
14
15  # Calculate the confidence interval
16  ci_lower = mean_sample - margin_of_error
17  ci_upper = mean_sample + margin_of_error
18
19  print(f"95% Confidence Interval for the mean: ({ci_lower}, {
        ci_upper})")
```

This code calculates and displays the 95% confidence interval for the population mean based on the previously generated sample.

Conclusions

Inference and parameter estimation are essential components of statistical analysis in artificial intelligence. Maximum likelihood estimation allows for optimal parameter estimates of a model, while constructing confidence intervals provides a methodology for quantifying the uncertainty of these estimates.

By understanding and applying these principles, practitioners can ground their analytical decisions in solid statistical foundations, thus improving the quality and trustworthiness of their models in the field of artificial intelligence. Constant practice with these tools will deepen knowledge and skills for making inferences in practical contexts.

## Chapter 20

Evaluation Methods in AI

Model evaluation is a crucial aspect in the development and application of artificial intelligence (AI) and machine learning systems. Without rigorous evaluation, it is difficult to know if a model is functioning as expected and if its results are reliable. This chapter will focus on various evaluation methods in AI, including accuracy metrics, the confusion matrix, and the ROC curve, among others. Through practical examples in Python, we aim to provide an in-depth understanding of how to effectively evaluate models.

Importance of Model Evaluation

Model evaluation allows developers and data scientists to:

- **Determine model effectiveness**: Knowing whether the model is making correct predictions.

- **Identify overfitting or underfitting**: Recognizing if the model is too tailored to the training data or not complex enough to capture the relationship in the data.

- **Compare different models**: Enabling comparison between different approaches and model configurations to decide which is most suitable for a specific task.

- **Tune hyperparameters**: Providing metrics for optimization and hyperparameter tuning during training.

Evaluation is particularly important because a model that appears to perform well on training data may fail to generalize to new data.

Evaluation Metrics

There are different evaluation metrics that can be applied, depending on the specific task (classification, regression, etc.). Let's start by reviewing some key metrics for classification problems, which are common in AI applications.

Accuracy

Accuracy is a metric indicating how many of the predictions made by the model are correct in relation to the total predictions made. It is calculated as:

$$\text{Accuracy} = \frac{\text{True Positives (TP)} + \text{True Negatives (TN)}}{\text{Total Examples}}$$

Accuracy provides an overview of the model's correctness, but it can be misleading in the case of imbalanced classes.

Recall (Sensitivity)

Recall or sensitivity measures the model's ability to detect all actual positive cases. It is calculated using the following formula:

$$Recall = \frac{\text{True Positives (TP)}}{\text{True Positives (TP)+False Negatives (FN)}}$$

A high recall indicates that few actual positive cases have been incorrectly classified as negative.

F1 Score

The **F1 score** is the harmonic mean between precision and recall. This metric is useful when there is an imbalance in class distribution, providing a middle ground between both metrics. It is expressed as:

$$F1 = 2 \cdot \frac{\text{Precision·Recall}}{\text{Precision+Recall}}$$

A high F1 score suggests that the model is balancing both precision and recall well.

Confusion Matrix

The **confusion matrix** is a tool that provides more details about the model's performance, showing true positives, true negatives, false positives, and false negatives. It is commonly used to evaluate classification models.

Example of Confusion Matrix

Suppose we are developing a model to classify emails as "spam" or "not spam." After making predictions with our model, we may find the following results:

	Predicted Spam	Predicted Not Spam
Actual Spam	TP (30)	FN (5)
Actual Not Spam	FP (3)	TN (62)

Using these values, we can calculate evaluation metrics, including accuracy, recall, and F1 score.

Implementation in Python

Let's implement the confusion matrix and calculate the relevant metrics in Python using scikit-learn.

```python
from sklearn.metrics import confusion_matrix,
    classification_report
import numpy as np

# True labels and model predictions
y_true = np.array(['spam', 'spam', 'no spam', 'no spam',
    'spam', 'spam', 'no spam', 'no spam', 'spam', 'no spam'])
y_pred = np.array(['spam', 'no spam', 'spam', 'no spam',
    'spam', 'spam', 'no spam', 'spam', 'spam', 'no spam'])

# Calculate confusion matrix
cm = confusion_matrix(y_true, y_pred, labels=['spam',
    'no spam'])
print("Confusion Matrix:\n", cm)

# Classification report
report = classification_report(y_true, y_pred, target_names
    =['spam', 'no spam'])
print("Classification Report:\n", report)
```

This code will calculate the confusion matrix and generate a detailed report that includes accuracy, recall, and F1 score.

ROC Curve and AUC

The **ROC curve** (Receiver Operating Characteristic) is a graphical representation that shows the true positive rate against the false positive rate at various decision thresholds. It is useful to evaluate the performance of a binary classification model, especially when the positive class is rare.

The area under the ROC curve (AUC - Area Under Curve) is a metric that quantifies the quality of the classifier. An AUC of 1.0 indicates a perfect model, while an AUC of 0.5 indicates performance similar to random guessing.

Example of ROC Curve

Let's see how to implement the ROC curve in Python using `scikit-learn`:

```python
import matplotlib.pyplot as plt
from sklearn.metrics import roc_curve, auc

# True values and classification probabilities
y_true_binary = np.array([1, 1, 0, 0, 1, 1, 0, 0, 1, 0])
# 1 = spam, 0 = not spam
y_scores = np.array([0.9, 0.85, 0.1, 0.4, 0.75, 0.8, 0.2, 0.5, 0.95, 0.3])  # Predicted probabilities

# Calculate ROC curve
fpr, tpr, thresholds = roc_curve(y_true_binary, y_scores)
roc_auc = auc(fpr, tpr)

# Plot ROC curve
plt.figure(figsize=(8, 5))
```

```
14  plt.plot(fpr, tpr, color='blue', label=f'AUC = {roc_auc:.2f
    }')
15  plt.plot([0, 1], [0, 1], color='red', linestyle='--')
    # Diagonal line
16  plt.title('ROC Curve')
17  plt.xlabel('False Positive Rate')
18  plt.ylabel('True Positive Rate')
19  plt.legend()
20  plt.grid()
21  plt.show()
```

In this code snippet, we generate an ROC curve for a spam/not spam classifier, showing its true and false positive rates at different thresholds.

Evaluation of Regression Models

For regression tasks, different metrics are used, which are essential for measuring the performance of a regression model.

Mean Squared Error (MSE)

The **mean squared error (MSE)** measures the average of the squared errors between the observed values and the predicted values. It is computed as follows:

$$MSE = \frac{1}{n} \sum_{i=1}^{n} (y_i - \hat{y}_i)^2$$

A MSE close to zero indicates that the model is making good predictions.

Root Mean Squared Error (RMSE)

The **root mean squared error (RMSE)** is the square root of the MSE and provides a measure of error in the same units as the predicted variable:

$$RMSE = \sqrt{MSE}$$

R² (Coefficient of Determination)

The **coefficients of determination (R^2)** quantifies the proportion of the variance in the dependent variable that can be explained by the independent variables in the model. It is calculated as:

$$R^2 = 1 - \frac{SS_{res}}{SS_{tot}}$$

where SS_{res} is the sum of squares of the residuals and SS_{tot} is the total sum of squares.

Example of Regression Evaluation

Imagine we have built a linear regression model and want to evaluate its performance using the mentioned metrics. Here is an example in Python:

```
1  from sklearn.metrics import mean_squared_error, r2_score
2
3  # True values and model predictions
4  y_true_reg = np.array([3, -0.5, 2, 7])
5  y_pred_reg = np.array([2.5, 0.0, 2, 8])
6
7  # Calculate MSE and R²
8  mse_reg = mean_squared_error(y_true_reg, y_pred_reg)
```

```
 9  rmse_reg = np.sqrt(mse_reg)
10  r2_reg = r2_score(y_true_reg, y_pred_reg)
11
12  print(f"Mean Squared Error (MSE): {mse_reg}")
13  print(f"Root Mean Squared Error (RMSE): {rmse_reg}")
14  print(f"Coefficient of Determination (R²): {r2_reg}")
```

This code will calculate the MSE, RMSE, and R² for a small set of true values and predictions from a regression model.

Final Considerations

Model evaluation is a fundamental process in the development of artificial intelligence and machine learning. From accuracy and recall to the ROC curve and regression metrics, it is essential to understand and apply the appropriate metrics to evaluate model performance.

As AI systems continue to evolve and face new challenges, reviewing and refining evaluation methods will ensure that these systems are robust, accurate, and reliable. Regular practice and case study analysis will help professionals develop a deep understanding of model evaluation and apply these skills in the real world.

## Chapter 21

Introduction to Information Theory

Information theory is a fundamental branch of mathematics and computing that deals with the quantification, storage, and communication of information. In the context of artificial intelligence (AI), information theory plays a crucial role in analyzing and understanding data, as well as in the design of machine learning algorithms. Throughout this chapter, we will explore key concepts of information theory, such as entropy, mutual information, and their applicability to AI problems.

What is Information

Before diving into information theory, it is important to define what we mean by "information." In general terms, information is a set of data that reduces uncertainty about an event or state of the world. The more information we have about a phenomenon, the lower the associated uncertainty.

For example, if we roll a six-sided die, the probability of rolling a specific number is 1/6. If we also know that an odd number has come up, our uncertainty decreases significantly, as there are now only three possible outcomes (1, 3, or 5).

Entropy: Measure of Uncertainty

The concept of **entropy** is fundamental in information theory. Introduced by Claude Shannon in his seminal 1948 paper, entropy measures the uncertainty or the amount of information contained in a random variable. It is formally expressed as:

$$H(X) = -\sum_{i=1}^{n} p(x_i) \log p(x_i)$$

where $H(X)$ is the entropy of the random variable X, x_i are the possible outcomes, and $p(x_i)$ is the probability of each outcome.

Example of Entropy

Consider a fair six-sided die. The entropy of rolling this die can be calculated as follows:

- For a fair die, each face has the same probability $p(x_i) = \frac{1}{6}$.

Now, substituting into the entropy formula:

$$H(X) = -\sum_{i=1}^{6} \frac{1}{6} \log \left(\frac{1}{6}\right) = -6 \left(\frac{1}{6} \log \left(\frac{1}{6}\right)\right) = -\log \left(\frac{1}{6}\right)$$

Using a base 2 logarithm, the numerical calculation gives us:

$$H(X) \approx 2.585 \text{ bits}$$

This means that we need approximately 2.585 bits of information to describe the outcome of rolling a die.

Mutual Information: Relationship Between Two Variables

Mutual information measures how much the information from one variable can predict the information of another variable. In simpler terms, it can be understood as the reduction in uncertainty of one variable given the other variable. It is calculated as:

$$I(X; Y) = H(X) + H(Y) - H(X, Y)$$

where:

- $I(X; Y)$ is the mutual information between variables X and Y.
- $H(X)$ and $H(Y)$ are the entropies of X and Y, respectively.
- $H(X, Y)$ is the joint entropy of X and Y.

Example of Mutual Information

Let's imagine two variables; X, representing the weather (Sunny, Cloudy, Rainy), and Y, representing whether an umbrella is taken (Yes, No). As we calculate the mutual information between these two variables, we might observe that:

- A sunny day likely does not require an umbrella, while a rainy day would require one.
- If we know it is cloudy, there is still uncertainty regarding whether an umbrella will be used.

Calculating the mutual information would yield a number that reflects how much the weather variable helps predict the use of an umbrella. If mutual information is high, it means that having knowledge about the weather significantly reduces uncertainty about whether or not to take an umbrella.

Applications of Information Theory in AI

Information theory has multiple applications in the field of artificial intelligence and machine learning. Some of the most prominent applications include:

Feature Selection

Mutual information is commonly used for **feature selection** in machine learning models. Selecting features that provide the most information reduces the dimensionality of the problem and improves model performance by eliminating irrelevant variables that could introduce noise.

Learning Algorithms

Some machine learning algorithms, such as decision trees, use entropy and mutual information as criteria for splitting nodes. By choosing the feature that offers the maximum information gain, decision trees can effectively classify data following the most informative decisions.

Data Compression

Information theory also finds application in **data compression**. Understanding the amount of information necessary to represent a dataset allows for the development of efficient compression methods that minimize space usage without significant loss of information.

Game Theory

In game theory, information plays a crucial role in analyzing strategic decisions. Information, viewed in the context of information theory, can help evaluate how the presence or absence of information affects the decisions of participants.

Conclusions

Throughout this chapter, we have explored the fundamental concepts of information theory, including entropy and mutual information. These concepts not only allow us to quantify uncertainty in various contexts but also provide practical tools for designing and evaluating algorithms in artificial intelligence.

As AI systems continue to evolve and face more complex challenges, information theory will remain a fundamental part of the analysis and development of new solutions that enhance data understanding and optimize decision-making. Through a solid understanding of information theory, professionals can build more robust and efficient models, taking AI to new heights in its applicability and potential.

## Chapter 22

Bayesian Networks and Their Applications

Bayesian networks are graphical probabilistic models that represent a set of variables and their conditional dependencies through a directed acyclic graph. These structures are extremely useful in various fields such as artificial intelligence, statistics, medicine, and economics, due to their ability to effectively model uncertainties and make inferences from incomplete or uncertain data. In this chapter, we will explore the fundamental concepts of Bayesian networks, their structure, how they are constructed, and how they can be applied to real-world problems, accompanied by practical examples in Python.

Introduction to Bayesian Networks

Bayesian networks are based on the **Bayesian theory** of probability, which allows us to update our beliefs about a variable as we obtain new information. They consist of nodes and arcs, where each node represents a random variable and the arcs indicate probabilistic dependency relationships between them.

Key Concepts

1. **Random Variables**: Each node in the network represents a variable, which can be discrete (such as "rain" yes/no) or continuous (such as "temperature").

2. **Conditional Dependencies**: The connections between nodes indicate that the probability of a node depends on one or more parent nodes. For example, in a Bayesian network modeling the weather, the probability of carrying an umbrella may depend on whether it is raining or not.

3. **Probability Distributions**: Associated with each node is a distribution that describes the probability of the variable taking a specific value given its parent nodes.

Structure of a Bayesian Network

The structure of a Bayesian network can be graphically represented. To illustrate, let's consider a simple network including three variables: "Weather", "Rain", and "Umbrella". The network can be represented as follows:

```
Weather -> Rain -> Umbrella
```

The interpretation is clear: the weather affects the rain, which in turn affects whether a person decides to carry an umbrella.

Probability Matrices

To build a Bayesian network, our next step is to define the probability distributions associated with each node. For the variable "Rain", we could have a conditional probability table (CPT) that looks like this:

Weather	Probability of Rain
Sunny	0.1
Cloudy	0.5
Rainy	0.8

With this table, we can define the probability of rain based on weather conditions. For the "Umbrella", the distribution might be:

Rain	Probability of Umbrella
No	0.2
Yes	0.9

These tables are essential because they will help us calculate the probability of various configurations within the model.

Inference in Bayesian Networks

One of the most powerful functionalities of Bayesian networks is inference. Bayesian inference allows us to calculate the posterior probability of a variable given observed evidence from other variables. For example, if we know that "It is raining", what is the probability that the "Weather" is "Cloudy"?

Bayes' Theorem

Bayes' Theorem is the foundation of inference in Bayesian networks and is expressed as:

$$P(A \mid B) = \frac{P(B \mid A) \cdot P(A)}{P(B)}$$

Where:

- $P(A \mid B)$ is the posterior probability.

- $P(B \mid A)$ is the likelihood.

- $P(A)$ is the prior probability.

- $P(B)$ is the marginal probability.

This theorem allows us to update our beliefs upon observing new evidence.

Practical Inference Example

Let's use the `pgmpy` library, which is a powerful tool for working with Bayesian networks in Python, to create and infer from a simple Bayesian network. First, let's ensure that the library is installed:

```
1  pip install pgmpy
```

Next, let's construct our first Bayesian network:

```
1  from pgmpy.models import BayesianModel
2  from pgmpy.inference import VariableElimination
3  import pandas as pd
4
```

```
 5  # Definition of the Bayesian network
 6  model = BayesianModel([('Weather', 'Rain'), ('Rain',
    'Umbrella')])
 7
 8  # Definition of the probability distributions
 9  cpd_weather = pd.Series([0.3, 0.4, 0.3], index=['Sunny',
    'Cloudy', 'Rainy'])
10  cpd_rain = pd.DataFrame(data=[[0.1, 0.5, 0.8], [0.9, 0.5,
    0.2]],
11                             index=['No', 'Yes'],
12                             columns=['Sunny', 'Cloudy', 'Rainy'
    ])
13  cpd_umbrella = pd.DataFrame(data=[[0.2], [0.9]], index=[
    'No', 'Yes'], columns=['Rain'])
14
15  # Assign the distributions to the network
16  model.add_cpds(cpd_weather, cpd_rain, cpd_umbrella)
17
18  # Verify the validity of the model
19  assert model.check_model()
20
21  # Create an inferencer using variable elimination
22  inference = VariableElimination(model)
23
24
    # Question: What is the probability that "Rain" is "Yes"
    given that "Weather" is "Cloudy"?

25  posterior_rain = inference.query(variables=['Rain'],
    evidence={'Weather': 'Cloudy'})
26  print(posterior_rain)
```

In this code, we defined the structure of the Bayesian network, specified the probability distributions, and performed inference on the probability of rain given that the weather is cloudy. The query will return an object displaying the probabilities that the rain is "Yes" or "No".

Applications of Bayesian Networks

Bayesian networks are used in a variety of practical applications, such as:

1. **Medical Diagnosis**: They are used to model relationships between symptoms and diseases, allowing doctors to diagnose conditions based on the evidence presented.

2. **Recommendation Systems**: Systems can predict what products or services might interest a user based on the preferences of similar users.

3. **Failure Prediction**: In engineering, Bayesian networks help predict failures in mechanical or electronic systems, enabling the planning of preventive maintenance.

4. **Robotics**: They are used in decision-making where robots must make inferences about their environment based on noisy sensors.

5. **Finance**: Bayesian networks allow for modeling and managing risk, enabling financial professionals to assess investment scenarios.

Conclusion

Bayesian networks represent a powerful approach to modeling and reasoning under uncertainty. Their ability to combine different sources of information and update probabilities as new evidence is acquired makes them valuable tools in many application fields. As we continue to explore and delve into artificial intelligence, the use of Bayesian networks will remain a rich area for research and application.

Learning to build and work with Bayesian networks expands our analytical capabilities and enables us to make better decisions based on solid evidence and probabilistic methods. Therefore, it is essential for professionals and academics to not only familiarize themselves with these concepts but also to start applying them in their respective areas of work.

## Chapter 23

Improvement and Theorem Proving in AI

The improvement and proof of theorems are essential components in the development and validation of theories within the field of artificial intelligence (AI). While powerful AI models can produce impressive results, it is crucial that the theories behind these models are rigorously tested and grounded. This chapter will focus on proof techniques, the importance of theorem formalization, and how these concepts relate to AI practice.

Introduction to Theorem Proving

Theorem proving is a mathematical process that involves establishing the truth of a statement based on already accepted axioms and propositions. This process is fundamental to providing a logical and coherent framework upon which claims in AI can be based. Theorems serve as foundations upon which algorithms and models are developed, ensuring that the decisions made by these systems are justified.

Logical deduction can be performed in various ways, and the most common proof methods include:

- **Direct proof**: The theorem is established through a sequence of logical steps leading to the intended conclusion.

- **Proof by contradiction**: It is assumed that the theorem is false, and it is demonstrated that this assumption leads to a contradiction.

- **Mathematical induction**: Used to prove that a proposition is true for all natural numbers.

Importance of Theorem Formalization

The formalization of theorems is vital in AI for several reasons:

- **Clarity**: It allows claims to be more precise and less ambiguous, reducing the possibility of misunderstandings.

- **Validity**: It provides a formal method to prove the validity of new results, ensuring that algorithms and models are grounded in solid foundations.

- **Transferability**: Valid theorems can be utilized in different contexts, facilitating the development of new algorithms and approaches.

- **Continuous Improvement**: As new theorems are developed, they can be used to enhance and optimize existing models.

For instance, theorems addressing the convergence of machine learning algorithms ensure that under certain conditions, the algorithm will achieve optimal performance. This is fundamental to trusting the validity of a model deployed in production.

Proof Techniques

Let's examine some of the techniques commonly used in theorem proving and their application within the context of AI.

Direct Proof

Direct proof involves establishing the theorem through a logical sequence of steps. For example, when demonstrating the efficacy of an optimization algorithm, we could start from the properties of functions and the definition of the algorithm itself to arrive at the desired conclusion.

Practical Example: SGD Convergence Theorem

Stochastic Gradient Descent (SGD) is a popular algorithm in AI for minimizing loss functions. Consider the statement:

"SGD will converge to the local minimum of a differentiable function under certain conditions."

To prove this statement, we would assume that the function meets the conditions of convexity and continuity. From there, we would construct a series of steps confirming that each iteration of SGD reduces the value of the loss function.

Proof by Contradiction

Proof by contradiction is another effective technique. In this approach, one starts by assuming that the theorem they wish to prove is false and, through logical reasoning, arrives at a contradictory conclusion.

Practical Example: No Overfitting Theorem

Imagine we want to prove the theorem:

"A machine learning model cannot generalize effectively if it has too many parameters compared to the number of observations."

Let's assume that the model does generalize well. This would imply that the model has effectively learned from limited data. However, if it is indeed true that it has an excessive number of parameters, it could end up overfitting to the noise present in the data rather than capturing meaningful patterns. This results in a contradiction since it was initially established that the model generalizes well, which is falsely contradictory with the nature of overfitting. Thus, the theorem is proved.

Mathematical Induction

Mathematical induction is especially useful for establishing the truth of propositions in discrete contexts and problems related to series. In AI, it can be used to establish the correctness of iterative algorithms.

Practical Example: Recursive Algorithms

Consider a recursive algorithm that sorts data. The statement can be:

"The algorithm works correctly for any dataset of size n."

To apply induction, one would first prove that the algorithm works correctly for a base case (such as $n = 1$ or $n = 2$). Then, one would assume the algorithm works for $n = k$ and demonstrate that it also works for $n = k + 1$. This technique is common in the development of algorithms that require iterative correctness.

Practical Exercise: Proving a Simple Theorem

Let's see how to structure a proof using Python as a tool.

Theorem: *The sum of the first n integers is equal to* $\frac{n(n+1)}{2}$.

1. Verify the base case: $n = 1$.

2. Use the induction hypothesis: we will assume this is true for $n = k$

    .

3. Prove that it must be true for $n = k + 1$.

```
1   def sum_of_integers(n):
2       return n * (n + 1) // 2
3
4   # Base case
5   n = 1
6   assert sum_of_integers(n) == 1  # True
7
8   # Induction hypothesis
9   k = 3  # Example
10  assert sum_of_integers(k) == 6  # 3 + 2 + 1 = 6
11
12  # Prove that it must hold for k + 1
13  n = k + 1
14  assert sum_of_integers(n) == sum_of_integers(k) + n  # True
```

Conclusions

The improvement and proof of theorems are fundamental processes in the development of artificial intelligence. These methods allow us to establish the solidity of claims and ensure that the models and algorithms developed have robust logical and mathematical foundations. As we delve into the world of AI, it is essential to recognize the importance of these processes to ensure that the technologies implemented are effective and reliable.

By mastering proof techniques, we can not only advance our understanding of AI but also actively contribute to its evolution, creating increasingly robust and efficient models that can effectively tackle modern challenges.

Prediction and Modeling in Time Series Analysis

Time series analysis refers to the technique of analyzing sequential data, where the data is collected over time. From applications in finance and meteorology to monitoring production systems, forecasting in time series plays a fundamental role in artificial intelligence. This chapter will focus on the concepts and methods used for modeling and predicting in time series, as well as practical examples using Python.

Introduction to Time Series

A **time series** is a set of observations ordered in time. Time series can be simple, like daily temperatures, or complex, like stock prices over time. The main characteristic of time series is the dependence on time: the value at a given moment is related in some way to previous values.

Components of Time Series

Time series generally have four main components:

1. **Trend**: The general direction in which the series moves over the long term, whether upward, downward, or constant.

2. **Seasonality**: Fluctuations in the data that occur at regular intervals, such as product sales that increase during Christmas each year.

3. **Cycle**: Long-term behaviors that occur at irregular intervals, often influenced by economic factors or events.

4. **Noise**: Random and unpredictable variations that cannot be modeled by other parts of the series.

Identifying these components is crucial for building suitable forecasting models.

Methods for Time Series Analysis

There are different approaches and techniques for analyzing and modeling time series. This chapter will discuss two of the most commonly used methods: ARIMA models and exponential smoothing models.

ARIMA Models

The **ARIMA** (Autoregressive Integrated Moving Average) model is one of the most popular approaches for time series forecasting. It is based on three components:

- **AR (Autoregressive)**: The relationship between the current interest and past values.

- **I (Integrated)**: Differentiation of the time series to make it stationary, i.e., removing trends and seasonality.

- **MA (Moving Average)**: The relationship between the current value and past errors.

Identifying the ARIMA Model

Before applying the ARIMA model, it is necessary to identify the order p, d, and q:

- **p** is the number of autoregressive terms.

- **d** is the number of differences needed to make the series stationary.

- **q** is the number of moving average terms.

This process can be guided using ACF (Autocorrelation Function) and PACF (Partial Autocorrelation Function) plots.

Practical Example of ARIMA

To illustrate the application of ARIMA, let's consider the analysis of daily temperature data. We will use Python and the `statsmodels` library.

```
1  import pandas as pd
2  import numpy as np
3  import matplotlib.pyplot as plt
4  from statsmodels.tsa.arima.model import ARIMA
5  from statsmodels.graphics.tsaplots import plot_acf,
     plot_pacf
```

```python
6
7  # Generate simulated temperature data
8  np.random.seed(42)
9  n_periods = 100
10 time = pd.date_range(start='2020-01-01', periods=n_periods,
   freq='D')
11 temperatures = np.random.normal(loc=20, scale=5, size=
   n_periods)
12 data = pd.Series(temperatures, index=time)
13
14 # Visualizing the time series
15 plt.figure(figsize=(10, 5))
16 plt.plot(data, label='Daily Temperatures')
17 plt.title('Time Series of Temperatures')
18 plt.xlabel('Date')
19 plt.ylabel('Temperature (°C)')
20 plt.legend()
21 plt.show()
22
23 # Autocorrelation analysis
24 plot_acf(data)
25 plt.show()
26
27 plot_pacf(data)
28 plt.show()
29
30 # Apply the ARIMA model
31 model = ARIMA(data, order=(2, 1, 1))
32 model_fit = model.fit()
33
34 # Prediction
35 forecast = model_fit.forecast(steps=10)
36 plt.figure(figsize=(10, 5))
37 plt.plot(data, label='Daily Temperatures')
38 plt.plot(pd.date_range(start='2020-04-11', periods=10, freq
```

```
   ='D'), forecast, label='Prediction')
39 plt.title('Temperature Prediction with ARIMA')
40 plt.xlabel('Date')
41 plt.ylabel('Temperature (°C)')
42 plt.legend()
43 plt.show()
```

In this example, we generated a simulated time series of daily temperatures, applied an ARIMA model, and made a prediction for the upcoming days.

Exponential Smoothing Models

Exponential smoothing is another valuable approach used to make predictions in time series. This method is based on the idea that the most recent observations are the most representative of future values. It is particularly used to forecast data with trend and seasonal components.

The most common models are:

1. **Simple Exponential Smoothing**: Used when there is no trend or seasonality.

2. **Holt's Exponential Smoothing**: An extension of simple smoothing that captures trends.

3. **Holt-Winters Exponential Smoothing**: Includes seasonal components.

Practical Example of Exponential Smoothing

Next, we will demonstrate how to apply the Holt-Winters exponential smoothing model in Python.

```python
from statsmodels.tsa.holtwinters import
ExponentialSmoothing

# Generate simulated data with trend and seasonality
np.random.seed(42)
time = pd.date_range(start='2020-01-01', periods=n_periods,
 freq='D')
seasonality = np.sin(np.linspace(0, 3.14 * 2, n_periods)) *
 5
trend = np.linspace(0, 10, n_periods)
data = pd.Series(trend + seasonality + np.random.normal(
scale=2, size=n_periods), index=time)

# Visualizing the time series
plt.figure(figsize=(10, 5))
plt.plot(data, label='Data with Trend and Seasonality')
plt.title('Time Series with Trend and Seasonality')
plt.xlabel('Date')
plt.ylabel('Value')
plt.legend()
plt.show()

# Apply the Holt-Winters model
model = ExponentialSmoothing(data, seasonal='add',
seasonal_periods=30)
model_fit = model.fit()

# Prediction
forecast = model_fit.forecast(steps=10)
plt.figure(figsize=(10, 5))
plt.plot(data, label='Original Data')
plt.plot(pd.date_range(start='2020-04-11', periods=10, freq
='D'), forecast, label='Prediction')
plt.title(
'Prediction with Holt-Winters Exponential Smoothing')
```

```
29  plt.xlabel('Date')
30  plt.ylabel('Value')
31  plt.legend()
32  plt.show()
```

In this code, we create a time series that includes trend and seasonal components and apply the Holt-Winters model to make future predictions.

Evaluation of Time Series Models

The evaluation of time series models is essential for validating the accuracy of our predictions. Some common metrics include:

- **Mean Squared Error (MSE)**: A measure that disproportionately penalizes large errors.

- **Root Mean Squared Error (RMSE)**: Provides a measure of error in the same units as the original data.

- **Mean Absolute Error (MAE)**: The average of the absolute differences between predictions and actual values.

These metrics not only allow for evaluating model performance but also for comparing different modeling approaches.

Conclusions

Time series analysis and forecasting are powerful tools in the arsenal of an artificial intelligence professional. Through techniques like ARIMA and exponential smoothing, it is possible to extract meaningful patterns and make inferences about future data, enabling informed decision-making across multiple fields.

By understanding the underlying components and applicable methods to time series, analysts can create accurate models tailored to the specific needs of their domain. This translates into an ability to anticipate events, optimize operations, and generate value from temporal data in a rapidly advancing world. As technology evolves, mastery of time series analysis will become increasingly essential for success in the field of artificial intelligence.

## Chapter 25

Combinatorics and Its Applications in AI

Combinatorics is a branch of mathematics that deals with studying and counting the possible configurations of a set of elements. Its relevance in the field of artificial intelligence (AI) lies in its ability to help solve complex problems related to optimization, search, and decision-making. In this chapter, we will explore fundamental concepts of combinatorics, as well as their practical applications in AI and specific examples that illustrate their utility.

Introduction to Combinatorics

Combinatorics primarily deals with two types of problems:

1. **Enumeration**: Counting the ways in which a set of elements can be grouped or arranged.

2. **Selection**: Determining the ways to choose elements from a set,

with or without repetition.

Some key concepts in combinatorics include:

- **Permutations**: The number of ways a set of n elements can be ordered. It is calculated using the formula:

$$P(n) = n!$$

where $n!$ (the factorial of n) is the product of the integers from 1 to n.

- **Combinations**: The ways in which r elements can be selected from a set of n elements, regardless of order. It is calculated using the formula:

$$C(n, r) = \frac{n!}{r!(n-r)!}$$

This formula works because it divides the total number of permutations by the permutations of the selected elements to avoid counting different orders.

- **Variations**: This refers to the number of ways in which a specific number of elements can be selected and ordered. The formula for variations is:

$$V(n, r) = \frac{n!}{(n-r)!}$$

Examples of Combinatorics

To better illustrate these concepts, let's see some practical examples using Python.

Permutations

Suppose we want to know how many ways we can organize the letters of the word "CAT". Since there are 4 different letters, we calculate the number of permutations:

```python
import math

# Calculate permutations
n = 4  # Number of letters in "CAT"
permutations = math.factorial(n)
print(f"Number of permutations of 'CAT': {permutations}")
```

The result will be 24, which is the number of ways to arrange the 4 letters of "CAT".

Combinations

Now, let's consider that we want to know how many ways we can select 2 letters from the word "CAT". We will use the combinations formula:

```python
# Calculate combinations
from math import comb

n = 4  # Total letters
r = 2  # Letters to select
combinations = comb(n, r)
print(f"Number of combinations of 2 letters from 'CAT': {
    combinations}")
```

The result will be 6, representing the possible combinations: "CA", "CT", "AT", "AC", "AT", and "TC".

Variations

Finally, let's calculate how many ways we can select and arrange 2 letters from "CAT":

```
1  # Calculate variations
2  def variations(n, r):
3      return math.factorial(n) // math.factorial(n - r)
4
5  variations_result = variations(n, r)
6  print(f"Number of variations of 2 letters from 'CAT': {
       variations_result}")
```

This will give us 12, which is the number of ways to select and arrange 2 letters from "CAT".

Applications of Combinatorics in AI

Combinatorics has multiple applications in the field of artificial intelligence. Below, we will discuss some areas where it is applied.

Resource Optimization

In many optimization problems, combinatorics is used to explore the space of possible solutions, identifying the best combination of resources. For example, when creating marketing strategies, it is essential to select which campaigns to launch and in what combination, and combinatorics allows for calculating all those options.

Search Problems

In designing search algorithms, such as those used in games or recommendation systems, combinatorics allows calculating how many possible configurations may exist. This is particularly applied in generating moves in strategy games, where evaluating potential combinations of moves and decisions is necessary.

Machine Learning

Feature selection in machine learning models often relies on combinations of different variables. Combinatorics helps determine the best features to use in model building, optimizing performance and reducing dimensionality.

Neural Networks

In training neural networks, combinatorics is also used to calculate the number of ways neurons can connect and activate. This directly affects the network's ability to learn complex data patterns.

Focus on Graph Theory

Within graph theory, combinatorics is fundamental for calculating the number of possible paths, cycles, or connections in networks. This approach is useful in social networks, logistics, and route optimization.

The Prince of Poincaré's Theorem

An interesting concept related to combinatorics is the Prince of Poincaré's theorem, which states that in any set of n elements, there will always be some combination of r elements that can be chosen, regardless of the order in which they are selected. This property directly relates to the applications discussed earlier, allowing linguistic or mathematical combinatorics to be applied to more complex analyses.

Conclusions

Combinatorics is an indispensable tool in the field of artificial intelligence. Through the enumeration and selection of possible configurations of elements, we can solve complex problems in optimization, search, and machine learning models. By understanding and applying combinatorial concepts, developers and researchers in AI can design more efficient algorithms and make informed decisions based on data combination analysis.

In a data-driven world, the ability to evaluate and explore combinations translates into competitive advantages and improvements in AI-based products and services. Therefore, it is essential to acquire a solid understanding to fully leverage the potential that combinatorics offers in this ever-evolving field.

## Chapter 26

Error Calculation and Sensitivity

In the context of artificial intelligence (AI), error calculation and sensitivity are crucial concepts for evaluating the performance of models. The quality of an AI model is not only measured by its accuracy but also by how well it responds to changes in input data and how it adapts to inherent variability. In this chapter, we will explore what errors are, how they are calculated, and the importance of sensitivity in evaluating AI models, including practical examples in Python.

Introduction to Error Calculation

In the field of artificial intelligence, an **error** refers to the difference between the values predicted by a model and the actual observed values. Understanding and calculating these errors is fundamental for improving prediction algorithms and ensuring they approach an optimal solution as closely as possible. This difference can be measured using various metrics, each with its own characteristics and advantages.

Types of Errors

There are several types of errors we can consider when evaluating AI models:

1. **Absolute Error**: This is the difference between the prediction and the actual value. It is calculated as: $\text{Absolute Error} = |y_{predicted} - y_{actual}|$

2. **Squared Error**: This type of error is calculated by squaring the difference between the prediction and the actual value. Its formula is: $\text{Squared Error} = (y_{predicted} - y_{actual})^2$

3. **Mean Squared Error (MSE)**: This is the average of the squared errors in a dataset. It is commonly used because it penalizes larger errors more: $MSE = \frac{1}{n}\sum_{i=1}^{n}(y_{predicted,i} - y_{actual,i})^2$

4. **Root Mean Squared Error (RMSE)**: This is the square root of the MSE and returns the average error in the same units as the data: $RMSE = \sqrt{MSE}$

5. **Mean Absolute Error (MAE)**: This is the average of the absolute errors: $MAE = \frac{1}{n}\sum_{i=1}^{n}|y_{predicted,i} - y_{actual,i}|$

Choosing the right metric depends on the type of problem we are facing, as each of them has different implications for model evaluation.

Practical Example of Error Calculation

Let's consider a practical case where we have a simple dataset with actual values and prediction models. Suppose our data is as follows:

- Actual Values: [3, -0.5, 2, 7]

- Predicted Values: [2.5, 0.0, 2, 8]

Now, let's calculate the absolute error, squared error, MSE, and RMSE using Python.

```python
import numpy as np

# Actual and predicted values
y_actual = np.array([3, -0.5, 2, 7])
y_predicted = np.array([2.5, 0.0, 2, 8])

# Calculate absolute error
absolute_error = np.abs(y_actual - y_predicted)
mse = np.mean((y_predicted - y_actual) ** 2)
rmse = np.sqrt(mse)
mae = np.mean(absolute_error)

# Results
print("Errors:")
print("Absolute Error:", absolute_error)
print("MSE:", mse)
print("RMSE:", rmse)
print("MAE:", mae)
```

Interpreting Results

The above code will give us results that allow us to evaluate the accuracy of our predictions compared to the actual values. We will calculate the absolute error at each data point, the mean squared error, and the RMSE. Depending on the results, we can adjust our model to improve its accuracy.

Sensitivity in AI Models

Sensitivity refers to a model's ability to respond to changes in input data. In an AI model, it is important to consider how sensitive the model is to variations in input parameters or noise in the data. Sensitivity provides vital information not only about the model's overall performance but also about its robustness.

Importance of Sensitivity

1. **Identification of Critical Parameters**: Sensitivity helps identify which variables have the greatest impact on the model's outcomes. This allows prioritizing efforts to improve data quality or adjust the modeling of certain variables.

2. **Model Robustness**: A model sensitive to small changes in the data may not be reliable in real-world scenarios. Evaluating the robustness of the model helps ensure that decisions based on predictions can be safely applied.

3. **Optimization**: Understanding how the variation of parameters influences the model's output provides valuable insights for optimizing model performance.

Sensitivity Example

Suppose we are working with a simple linear regression model. To evaluate its sensitivity, we will conduct a small experiment where we modify the input values and observe the impact on the output. Consider a simple linear function where:

$$y = mx + b$$

Where m is the slope and b is the intercept. Let's implement this in Python.

```python
1  import matplotlib.pyplot as plt
2
3  # Model data
4  x = np.array([1, 2, 3, 4, 5])
5  m = 2  # Slope
6  b = 1  # Intercept
7
8  # Initial prediction
9  y = m * x + b
10
11 plt.plot(x, y, label='Original Model')
12
13 # Study sensitivity with changes in slope
14 sensitivity_changes = [1.5, 2, 2.5]
15
16 for m in sensitivity_changes:
17     y_sensitivity = m * x + 1  # Fixed intercept
18     plt.plot(x, y_sensitivity, label=f'Model m={m}')
19
20 plt.title('Sensitivity in Linear Regression')
21 plt.xlabel('x')
22 plt.ylabel('y')
23 plt.legend()
24 plt.show()
```

Evaluating Model Sensitivity

From the graph, we observe how changes in the slope affect the linear relationship between x and y. By comparing the models, we can analyze whether the change in slope has a significant impact on the prediction and evaluate its relevance in real-world contexts.

Conclusions

Error calculation and sensitivity are fundamental elements in evaluating and optimizing artificial intelligence models. A solid understanding of how errors are calculated allows AI developers to improve the accuracy of their models, and the evaluation of sensitivity ensures that models are robust and reliable in the face of data variations.

As AI systems continue to evolve, the focus on error calculation and sensitivity evaluation will help advance toward more accurate and efficient models, which is essential in a world driven by data-based decisions. Ultimately, this understanding not only improves the quality of models but also ensures that AI is used ethically and effectively across multiple domains and applications.

Risk and Reliability Analysis

Risk and reliability analysis is a fundamental aspect of developing artificial intelligence (AI) systems and is highly relevant in decision-making across various industries, including engineering, healthcare, finance, and technology. As systems become more complex, understanding how to identify, assess, and mitigate risks becomes a critical skill for professionals in these fields. In this chapter, we will explore the key concepts of risk analysis, the methodologies used to assess the reliability of systems, and how they integrate into the development of AI-based solutions.

Introduction to Risk Analysis

Risk analysis involves the process of identifying, evaluating, and prioritizing the risks that may affect a project or system. In the context of AI, risks can arise from various factors, such as:

- Errors in machine learning algorithms.
- Poor quality or bias in training data.

- Security vulnerabilities in system deployment.

- Unexpected outcomes due to the model structure or its implementation.

Risks can translate into issues that are likely to affect the reliability, effectiveness, and ethics of the solution. Therefore, conducting a detailed analysis allows for better planning and preparation in the face of these inevitabilities.

Types of Risks

1. **Technical Risks**: Those related to the technologies themselves. These may include software failures, outdated hardware, or integration issues.

2. **Data Risks**: Focus on the quality and quantity of data, which can lead to a biased or ineffective model.

3. **Human Risks**: Refer to the possibility of human errors in data handling or in interpreting AI models.

4. **Regulatory Risks**: Regulations and standards that may change, affecting the viability and legality of the system.

5. **Reputational Risks**: Consequences arising from inappropriate outcomes or ethical violations that can damage the organization's image.

Framework for Risk Analysis

An effective framework for risk analysis in AI includes the following steps:

1. Risk Identification

The first step is to identify all possible risks that may arise during the project lifecycle. This often requires collaboration between interdisciplinary teams, such as engineers, data scientists, and legal experts.

Example: Risk Identification in a Facial Recognition Project

In a facial recognition project, some risks to consider may include:

- Bias in the training dataset that could affect the system's accuracy.
- Risk of privacy violations as user data is collected.
- Security vulnerabilities in the infrastructure that may compromise sensitive information.

2. Risk Assessment

Once identified, each risk must be assessed in terms of its likelihood of occurrence and the impact it would have. A risk matrix can be useful for visualizing this assessment.

Risk Matrix

Risk	Probability (1-5)	Impact (1-5)	Total Risk (P x I)
Bias in Training Data	4	5	20
Security	3	4	12

Risk	Probability (1-5)	Impact (1-5)	Total Risk (P x I)
Vulnerabilities			
Privacy Violation Risk	2	5	10

3. Risk Prioritization

Risks should be prioritized based on their total risk level (probability x impact). This allows teams to focus on managing the most critical risks first.

4. Risk Mitigation

The next step is to develop strategies to mitigate prioritized risks. Actions may include:

- Conducting thorough testing and validation on datasets to minimize biases.
- Implementing security systems and encryption to protect data.
- Establishing auditing and continuous monitoring processes to ensure the correct functioning of systems.

5. Monitoring and Review

Finally, it is crucial to continue monitoring the risks as the project evolves. New risks may arise, and existing ones may change in nature or severity, making periodic review essential.

Reliability Analysis

Reliability refers to a system's ability to perform under specified conditions for a defined period. In the context of AI, reliability implies that the model must provide consistent and accurate results over time.

Methods for Assessing Reliability

1. **Cross-Validation**: This involves dividing the dataset into several parts and then using different combinations of these parts to train and validate the model, ensuring performance is not dependent on a single partition of the dataset.

2. **A/B Testing**: Used to compare the effectiveness of two or more models or algorithms based on user interaction or performance.

3. **Simulation**: By using simulations, we can foresee how a system will respond to different conditions, assessing its reliability in scenarios that may not be covered in the training dataset.

Importance of Reliability in AI

Reliability is essential because:

- It ensures that the model behaves predictably.

- It fosters trust in the decisions made by the system.

- It reduces the risk of catastrophic failures in critical systems, such as those related to health or safety.

Example of Reliability Assessment

Suppose we are developing a model to predict product demand on an e-commerce site. We use cross-validation to assess the model's reliability:

```python
1  import pandas as pd
2  from sklearn.model_selection import cross_val_score
3  from sklearn.linear_model import LinearRegression
4
5  # Load data
6  data = pd.read_csv('demand_data.csv')
7  X = data[['feature1', 'feature2', 'feature3']]
8  y = data['demand']
9
10 # Model and cross-validation
11 model = LinearRegression()
12 scores = cross_val_score(model, X, y, cv=5)
       # 5-fold cross-validation
13
14 print(f'Accuracies for each fold: {scores}')
15 print(f'Mean accuracy: {scores.mean()}')
```

In this example, we validate a linear regression model using cross-validation and check its accuracy across different parts of the dataset, providing a better understanding of its reliability.

Conclusions

Risk analysis and reliability assessment are critical components in the development and application of artificial intelligence technologies. As these systems become more integrated into everyday life, ensuring they operate safely and effectively becomes a priority. A solid understanding of risk analysis methods and reliability not only enhances the performance of AI models but also strengthens user trust in these critical technologies.

As professionals in the field, it is our responsibility to identify and mitigate risks, preserve system integrity, and ensure that AI solutions are deployed ethically and responsibly. In an information-driven world, the ability to conduct effective risk analysis and evaluate the reliability of systems will be essential for the ongoing success of artificial intelligence applications.

## Chapter 28

Stochastic Optimization in AI Models

Stochastic optimization is a crucial approach in the field of artificial intelligence (AI), particularly in optimizing algorithms and models that must handle uncertainties and variations in data. As AI systems become more complex and face real-world problems, the ability to optimize under stochastic conditions becomes increasingly important. In this chapter, we will explore the fundamentals of stochastic optimization, its methods, applications, and practical examples in Python.

Introduction to Stochastic Optimization

Stochastic optimization refers to a set of techniques used to find the best solutions to problems where there is uncertainty or variability in the data. In contrast to deterministic optimization, where all parameters and variables are known and fixed, stochastic optimization considers that some of these may vary.

This approach is particularly relevant in contexts where data may be noisy, where cost functions may be nonlinear and complex, and in situations where decisions must be made dynamically over time.

Example of Stochastic Context

Imagine you are trying to train a machine learning model to predict the demand for a product over a certain period. You have a set of historical data, but actual demand is hard to predict due to external factors such as weather changes, marketing events, or competition. Here, the uncertainty in the input data makes stochastic optimization an appropriate approach, as it allows for continuous adjustments to the model based on observed variability.

Stochastic Optimization Methods

There are several methods in stochastic optimization, each with its own characteristics and approaches to handling uncertainty. We will discuss some of the most common methods in this chapter.

Stochastic Gradient

Stochastic Gradient Descent (SGD) is one of the most commonly used algorithms in stochastic optimization. It is a variant of the classic gradient method where only a random subset of data (or a "mini-batch") is used to compute the updates of the optimization variable at each iteration.

The idea behind SGD is that by working with random examples instead of the entire dataset, the process can converge faster, and in some cases, it may avoid getting trapped in locally suboptimal solutions. However, this random nature also means that noise is introduced in the updates, which can lead to fluctuations in the cost function.

Stochastic Gradient Equation

The parameter update in SGD can be expressed by the following formula: $\theta_t = \theta_{t-1} - \eta \nabla J(\theta_{t-1}; X_t, y_t)$ where:

- θ_t are the model parameters at time t,
- η is the learning rate,
- J is the cost function,
- X_t and y_t are a random subset of input and output data.

Evolutionary Algorithms

Evolutionary algorithms are a set of techniques inspired by the process of natural evolution, using concepts such as selection, reproduction, and mutation to explore the solution space. These methods are particularly useful for solving complex and nonlinear optimization problems where the search space may be very large.

Some of the most widely used evolutionary algorithms include:

- **Genetic Algorithms**: These are based on the principle of survival of the fittest, utilizing a population of solutions that evolve over generations.

- **Evolution Strategies**: These focus more on adaptation by modifying solutions in the population concerning their neighbors.

Example of Genetic Algorithms in Python

We can illustrate a simple genetic algorithm in Python where we try to maximize a function:

```python
import numpy as np

def fitness_function(x):
    return -x**2 + 4*x  # Function to maximize

def selection(population):
    scores = np.array([fitness_function(ind) for ind in
    population])
    selected_indices = np.argsort(scores)[-2:]
    # Select the two best
    return population[selected_indices]

def crossover(parent1, parent2):
    return (parent1 + parent2) / 2
    # Crossover by averaging

def mutation(ind):
    return ind + np.random.normal(0, 0.1)
    # Add a little noise

# Population initialization
population_size = 10
population = np.random.uniform(0, 5, population_size)

# Evolution process
for generation in range(10):
    new_population = []
    selected_parents = selection(population)

    for _ in range(population_size):
        if np.random.rand() < 0.5:
    # Select between parents
            offspring = crossover(selected_parents[0],
    selected_parents[1])
            offspring = mutation(offspring)
```

```
30              new_population.append(offspring)
31
32      population = np.array(new_population)
33
34  print("Best solution found:", population[np.argmax([
    fitness_function(ind) for ind in population])])
```

Monte Carlo Methods

Monte Carlo methods are a class of algorithms that use random simulations to solve complex mathematical problems. These methods are particularly useful in situations where it is difficult or impossible to develop an analytical model.

In the context of optimization, Monte Carlo algorithms can be used to explore the possible solution space, estimate the expected value of a solution, and help make optimal decisions under uncertainty.

Example of Monte Carlo Method in Python

Imagine we want to assess the risk of a financial asset. We can use the Monte Carlo method to simulate different possible outcomes:

```
1  import numpy as np
2  import matplotlib.pyplot as plt
3
4  def monte_carlo_simulation(steps=100, simulations=1000):
5      results = []
6
7      for _ in range(simulations):
8          price = 100  # Initial price
```

```
 9            for _ in range(steps):
10                daily_return = np.random.normal(0, 0.01)
   # Simulated daily return
11                price *= (1 + daily_return)
12            results.append(price)
13
14      return results
15
16  # Simulations
17  simulated_prices = monte_carlo_simulation()
18  plt.hist(simulated_prices, bins=50)
19  plt.title("Distribution of Simulated Prices")
20  plt.xlabel("Final Price")
21  plt.ylabel("Frequency")
22  plt.show()
```

Applications of Stochastic Optimization

Stochastic optimization has applications in numerous fields within artificial intelligence:

1. **Machine Learning**: Optimizing the weights in neural networks is often carried out using stochastic methods to find the optimal configurations that minimize the loss function.

2. **Robotics**: In the planning and control of robots, stochastic algorithms enable robots to adapt their actions based on feedback from their variable environment.

3. **Economics and Finance**: They are used in portfolio management, where uncertainty in asset returns makes it necessary to optimize stochastically.

4. **Transportation Networks**: Optimizing routes in logistics and

transportation, where traffic and weather conditions are variables that affect the best decision to make.

Challenges in Stochastic Optimization

Despite its capabilities, stochastic optimization presents certain challenges:

- **Convergence**: Ensuring that methods converge to an optimal solution can be complicated due to the noise and inherent variability in the data.

- **Computation Time**: Stochastic methods, especially those relying on simulations like Monte Carlo, can require significant computation time.

- **Overfitting**: There is a risk that models may overfit the variability of noise in the data if not handled properly.

Conclusions

Stochastic optimization is a fundamental tool in artificial intelligence that enables the development of robust and adaptable models to changes and uncertainties in data. Through methods like stochastic gradient descent, evolutionary algorithms, and Monte Carlo methods, data scientists can find optimal solutions in complex and dynamic contexts.

With the growth of data and the proliferation of AI systems, mastering stochastic optimization not only improves model effectiveness but also ensures that they are resilient and reliable across multiple applications. Understanding these techniques will enable professionals to tackle emerging challenges and continue advancing the design of effective and efficient solutions in an increasingly uncertain world.

## Chapter 29

Ethics and Considerations in the Mathematical Application of AI

Artificial Intelligence (AI) has revolutionized multiple sectors, from healthcare to finance, driving efficiency and innovation. However, with its growing adoption, there emerges a need to address the ethical and accountability issues that arise from its use. In this chapter, we will explore ethics in AI focusing on mathematical applications, the challenges presented, and the considerations that must be taken into account to ensure responsible development and use.

Introduction to Ethics in AI

Ethics in AI refers to the norms and principles that should guide the development, implementation, and use of artificial intelligence systems. The impact these systems can have on people's lives and society at large demands a cautious and responsible approach. The fact that AI is based on mathematical models and complex algorithms does not exempt developers and organizations from considering what is morally right and just.

Common Ethical Dilemmas

In the realm of AI, several ethical dilemmas arise that deserve attention:

- **Algorithmic Bias**: AI-based models can perpetuate or even amplify existing biases in training data, resulting in unfair or discriminatory decisions. This is critical in applications such as personnel recruitment, loan granting, or law enforcement.

- **Transparency and Explainability**: Many AI models, especially those that use deep learning, can be considered "black boxes." This means that it is difficult, if not impossible, to understand how they make decisions. The lack of explanations for predictions raises concerns about trust and accountability.

- **Data Privacy and Security**: The collection and use of large volumes of data raise issues regarding individuals' privacy. Using data without consent or in ways that users do not anticipate can have serious consequences.

- **Autonomy and Accountability**: With the rise of autonomous systems, such as self-driving vehicles or virtual assistants, the question arises of who is responsible for the decisions made by AI in critical situations.

Mathematical Applications and Ethical Considerations

As we explore the mathematical applications behind AI, it is essential to take into account the associated ethical considerations. Some of the key areas where mathematics plays a crucial role are:

Machine Learning Algorithms

Machine learning algorithms utilize mathematical techniques to learn patterns from data. It is fundamental that the datasets used to train these models are representative and free of biases. Otherwise, the resulting models may discriminate against certain groups.

Example of Bias in Algorithms

Consider an algorithm designed to predict credit risk based on historical data. If the dataset contains racial bias (for example, if certain demographic groups have been historically penalized), the model may incorrectly label individuals from those groups as higher risk. This results in the denial of credit to individuals who would otherwise be solvent.

Neural Networks

Neural networks, especially those with many layers (deep learning), are powerful but complex. Their ability to learn abstract features also makes them difficult to interpret. This is where the importance of explainability comes into play.

The Need for Transparency

As a model becomes more complex, the ability to understand its workings diminishes. This raises an ethical question: should we trust a model that we cannot explain? The research community is working on methods to make "black box" models more interpretable, using techniques like layer activation visualization and the use of intrinsically simpler models for comparison.

Privacy in Data Handling

Manipulating large volumes of data often requires a significant amount of personal information, raising serious privacy concerns. The mathematics applied in AI often relies on data that could infringe upon individuals' rights.

Example: Personal Data Analysis

Imagine a recommendation system that uses previous purchase data from users. If this data has not been anonymized or properly handled, it could reveal sensitive information about individuals' purchasing habits, exposing their preferences and behaviors.

Approaches for Data Protection

It is essential to implement a privacy-focused approach, such as differential privacy, which allows for data analysis while protecting individuals' identities. With this method, individual data contributions are distorted in such a way that general inferences can be made without compromising anyone's privacy.

Challenges in Implementing Ethical Principles

Implementing ethical principles in AI is not a simple task and faces several challenges:

- **Standards and Regulations**: The lack of a uniform regulatory framework and the diversity of laws and standards in different jurisdictions hinder the development of common policies around ethics in AI.

- **Commercial Interests**: Often, economic incentives can conflict with ethical practices. Companies may prioritize model performance over fairness and transparency due to competitive pressure.

- **Ignorance or Negligence**: Not all AI developers are aware of the ethical issues associated with their models or may choose to ignore them. Education on ethics in AI and adequate training is crucial to changing this attitude.

Pathways towards an Ethical Future in AI

To move towards a future where AI is used ethically and responsibly, it is essential to foster collaboration among different actors:

- **Ethics Education**: Including ethics in training and education programs in data science and AI development will ensure that professionals are equipped to make informed decisions.

- **Interdisciplinary Collaboration**: Involving experts in ethics, law, and sociology in the development of AI models will help identify potential ethical problems and design appropriate solutions.

- **Corporate Transparency**: Companies should be transparent about how they use and protect user data and about how their AI makes decisions, establishing a greater level of trust with consumers.

- **Development of Standards**: Creating standards and best practices can help guide organizations' efforts toward responsible and ethical AI implementation.

Conclusions

Artificial intelligence is transforming the world in multiple dimensions, and the underlying mathematics drives this revolution. However, the benefits of AI cannot be achieved at the expense of ethics. The need for a responsible approach in the development and implementation of AI solutions is paramount. Through critical reflection and conscious action, we can use mathematics and AI to create systems that ultimately benefit society in a fair and equitable manner.

As we reflect on the ethics and considerations in the mathematical application of AI, let us remember that technology should serve the common good, prioritizing fairness, transparency, and accountability. Only then can we ensure that AI is not merely a powerful tool but also a beacon of ethical and social progress.

## Chapter 30

Future Trends and Challenges in AI Mathematics

Artificial intelligence (AI) continues to evolve at an unprecedented pace, with mathematics being its beating heart. Understanding future trends in mathematics related to AI is essential for anyone looking to engage in this dynamic and ever-changing field. This chapter discusses emerging trends and challenges faced by the scientific and technological community, in an effort to pave the way for a future where AI is more effective, ethical, and accessible.

Introduction to Trends in AI Mathematics

Mathematics underpins almost every aspect of artificial intelligence, from algorithm optimization to data representation and machine learning. Mathematical trends play a significant role in how AI techniques are developed and applied. As the complexity of systems grows, it is evident that mathematics needs to evolve to address new challenges.

Intersection of Mathematics and Deep Learning

One of the most notable trends in the field of AI is the explosive growth of deep learning, which relies heavily on concepts from linear algebra, calculus, and probability theory. Neural network architectures have become increasingly complex, requiring advanced mathematics for their analysis and interpretation.

Evolution of Architectures

From convolutional neural networks (CNNs) for computer vision tasks to recurrent neural networks (RNNs) for natural language processing, these architectures have not only improved in terms of performance but have also expanded the range of applications. New architectures like Transformers, which power many modern natural language processing systems, have introduced novel mathematical concepts that are at the forefront of AI research.

Interpretable Machine Learning Algorithms

Another rising trend is the demand for machine learning models that are interpretable and explainable. While AI models like decision trees are relatively easy to understand, other more complex models, such as deep neural networks, can be considered "black boxes." The community has begun exploring mathematical ways to clarify how and why decisions are made, using approaches like LIME (Local Interpretable Model-agnostic Explanations) and SHAP (SHapley Additive exPlanations).

Advances in Game Theory and AI

Game theory has seen a significant resurgence in the context of AI.

Interactions among autonomous agents, especially in multi-agent systems, present complex challenges that require advanced mathematical tools. Optimization in competitive environments, negotiation among agents, and mechanism design are becoming increasingly relevant in sectors like finance and robotics.

Challenges in AI Mathematics

Despite the exciting trends, challenges loom on the horizon. Some of the most critical challenges include resource allocation, model scalability, data quality and quantity, and, of course, the ethical dilemmas surrounding AI.

Scalability of AI Models

Scalability is a key challenge facing the AI community in terms of mathematical structures. As more complex models with multiple layers and neurons are developed, computational costs skyrocket. This challenge requires creating more efficient algorithms and the mathematical development of techniques such as parallelization of calculations and implementation of stochastic optimization algorithms.

Example of Scalability

Imagine we are training a deep neural network with millions of parameters. The training time could exponentially increase if traditional methods are used. Instead, we might implement the Adam optimization algorithm, which improves efficiency by dynamically adjusting learning rates during training, thereby contributing to its scalability.

```
1   import tensorflow as tf
```

```
 2  from tensorflow.keras import layers, models
 3
 4  # Define an example neural network
 5  model = models.Sequential([
 6      layers.Dense(64, activation='relu', input_shape=(
        input_dim,)),
 7      layers.Dense(64, activation='relu'),
 8      layers.Dense(32, activation='relu'),
 9      layers.Dense(output_dim, activation='softmax'),
10  ])
11
12  # Compile the model using the Adam optimizer
13  model.compile(optimizer='adam',
14                loss='categorical_crossentropy',
15                metrics=['accuracy'])
```

Data Quality and Quantity

Another significant difficulty is the quality and quantity of the data feeding the AI models. There is a delicate balance between having access to large volumes of data and ensuring that such data is of high quality, representative, and unbiased. Mathematics plays a crucial role in data preprocessing through techniques like normalization and outlier removal.

Data Preprocessing in Python

Here is an example of how Python can be used to prepare data before it is introduced into an AI model, utilizing the Pandas library:

```
 1  import pandas as pd
 2
```

```
3   # Load the dataset
4   data = pd.read_csv('data.csv')
5
6   # Inspect for missing data
7   print(data.isnull().sum())
8
9   # Impute missing data with the mean
10  data.fillna(data.mean(), inplace=True)
11
12  # Normalize the data
13  from sklearn.preprocessing import StandardScaler
14  scaler = StandardScaler()
15  data_scaled = scaler.fit_transform(data)
```

Ethical Dilemmas and Responsibilities

Lastly, the ethical dilemma and responsibility in the use of mathematics in AI are perhaps the most pressing challenge. With issues like bias in datasets and lack of interpretability in models, ensuring that decisions made by AI systems are based on solid ethical principles is essential.

Ethical Reflections

Mathematics can shape these ethical issues. For example, when developing algorithms that assess credit risk, the use of sensitive variables (such as race or gender) must be carefully examined. Implementing regulations and ethical frameworks may be vital for defusing these dilemmas and ensuring that AI operates fairly and equitably.

Future Trends: A Collaborative Future

As we move toward the future, collaboration among mathematicians, data scientists, and AI experts becomes vital. Communities must come together to tackle the challenges of machine learning and applied mathematics.

Combined Innovations

One possible future trend is the combination of machine learning techniques with mathematical concepts from other disciplines, such as physics and biology. This could lead to the development of new algorithms that solve complex problems more effectively and efficiently.

Interdisciplinarity

Interdisciplinary research may result in innovative approaches to complex problems. For instance, utilizing principles from quantum physics in the development of AI algorithms could open a new field where quantum computing intersects with machine learning.

Conclusions

Mathematics is foundational for the development and implementation of artificial intelligence. As the field progresses, staying informed about trends in applied mathematics, as well as the challenges facing this discipline, is essential. Preparing for the future will involve a commitment to ethical, interpretable, and collaborative solutions in AI mathematics. This chapter has explored a dynamic and frequently changing landscape, suggesting that the future of AI relies not just on code and data, but also on a solid mathematical foundation.

As artificial intelligence deploys across various sectors and in our daily lives, it becomes evident that a responsible approach to AI mathematics will not only benefit the industry but also society as a whole.

www.ingramcontent.com/pod-product-compliance
Lightning Source LLC
LaVergne TN
LVHW051321050326
832903LV00031B/3292

* 9 7 9 8 3 1 5 3 4 1 1 3 0 *